Life's Highest Blessings

The Mahā Maṅgala Sutta

Translation and Commentary
by
Dr. R. L. Soni

Revised by
Bhikkhu Khantipālo

Buddhist Publication Society
P.O. Box 61,
54, Sangharaja Mawatha,
Kandy, Sri Lanka.

First BPS edition: 1978
Reprinted: 1987, 2012

National Library and Documentation Services Board -
Cataloguing-In-Publication Data

Tripitaka. Sutrapitaka
Maha mangala sutta: Life's Highest Blessings / R.L. Soni; ed. by Bhikkhu Khantipalo.- Kandy: Buddhist Publication Society Inc.., 2012. BP 432S. - 94p.; 12.5cm
ISBN 978-955-24-0392-7

i. 294.3823 DDC23 ii. Title
iii. Soni, R.L.
iv. Bhikkhu Khantipalo ed.

1. Sutrapitaka
2. Tripitaka
3. Buddhism

ISBN: 978-955-24-0392-7

Cover art by Mr. Charith Weerasena

Printed by
Creative Printers & Designers,
Bahirawakanda, Kandy.

EDITOR'S FOREWORD

MAṄGALA: Popularly it means lucky sign, omen good or evil, auspicious or inauspicious, or a blessing. In all countries and times there have been superstitions about these things and this is as true of Western technological societies (the increasing dependence upon astrology), as it was of India in the Buddha's days. Though people now may not divine auspices from the shapes of cloth nibbled by rats, they have plenty of other signs of fortune and misfortune.

For some reason or other, signs of fortune are few now in English tradition and offhand the writer could think of only one: it is lucky to pick up pins.[1] But unlucky signs and actions to ward off misfortune are many. For instance, a few years ago a sister in an English hospital insisted that flowers of other colours be mixed in with my mother's red and white carnations—"or we shall have a death in the ward." In Australia in the show biz world, to whistle in the dressing room before putting on an act will bring misfortune which can only be averted by leaving the room, turning round three times and swearing! Another generally unlucky sign is for a black cat to cross one's path. In Nepal, they consider an overturned shoe to be very inauspicious when one is setting out on a journey. And sailors the world over are well known for their attachment to good

1. Other "lucky" signs are: finding a four-leaved clover or a horseshoe, seeing a rainbow or a falling star a lady-bug landing one's body, and breaking a glass. (BPS editor)

signs and dread of ill omens. Less specialized examples can be found in crossing one's fingers and in "touching wood" against disaster, and in the practice of throwing salt over the left shoulder (into the Devil's eye) whenever salt is spilt. (Did salt manufacturers have anything to do with this?)

Certainly a well-known Swedish match company did promote the idea of ill-luck following three smokers who light up on one match ("three on a match"). A bit nearer to commonsense is the superstition about not walking under ladders, but most of these beliefs are quite irrational, like the children's idea that a bad day will follow after stepping on cracks in the pavement when going to school.

Even nearer to the Buddhist idea of good omens (in Thailand) are dreaming of Bhikkhus (monks) or temples, or seeing a Bhikkhu when one comes out of the house first thing in the morning. How such things can be interpreted differently is well illustrated by some Chinese business people for whom the sight of a Bhikkhu—one who teaches the doctrine of *voidness*—at that time is a very bad omen! In Theravāda countries generally the word "*sumaṅgala*" (= good omen) is a popular name both among Bhikkhus and laymen.

But one could keep on and find innumerable examples of the popular idea of *maṅgala*. It was the Buddha's genius to show that it is the practice of Dhamma that is truly auspicious.

In Buddhist countries there are many works explaining the contents of the Maṅgala Sutta. Some are in Pāli but many are in the languages of the present Buddhist countries of Southeast Asia. They are popular books widely read by Buddhists there. Apart from this, lectures over the radio and sermons in temples and homes often take the form of a commentary upon this discourse or part of it.

English language lacks such a work, apart from the translation of the Pāli commentary to the Sutta by the Venerable Ñāṇamoli Thera in *Minor Readings and Illustrator* (Pali Text Society). The author's book, written before this was available, helps to fill an omission in English Buddhist literature.

As the reviser of this book, I have often referred to Ven. Ñāṇamoli's translation and sometimes inserted some material from that book into this one. Where it was felt necessary some passages by the author have been omitted or rewritten. It is my hope that he will be satisfied with these changes, which do not affect the plan of his work. John Dimmick, my good Buddhist friend for many years, has patiently disentangled and typed the revised copy.

The Mahā Maṅgala Sutta is so popular because of the wide range of its teaching within a few easily remembered verses. Also because of its clarity and straightforwardness, which are characteristic of the Dhamma as a whole.

Here are good omens for everyone, real blessings for everybody. You have only to practice!

Bhikkhu Khantipālo

PREFACE

The Mahā Maṅgala Sutta is a rewarding text. In this work an attempt is made to offer some studies of this important discourse of the Buddha, which provides a plan, true at all times, for the material and spiritual well-being of individuals. The discourse provides lessons of direct practical application, capable of immediate and fruitful use by people in all walks of life, irrespective of differences of sex or status, race or religion.

The conditioning of the individual towards wholesome conduct is really necessary. Such a change of attitudes leads to definite improvement not only in domestic and social affairs but also in national and international ones. For the introduction and promotion of such friendliness, the auspicious words of the Buddha reaching us from across the ages provide an excellent guide.

The present work introduces this worthy guide and this book is sent out in the faith and hope that it will help lead some people in the world towards better human relationships.

Dr. R. L. Soni

CONTENTS

Editor's Foreword iii

Preface vi

Contents vii

Chapter I : Introduction 1
- I. The Glorious Sutta 1
- II. Location in the Scriptures 4
- III. The Contents of These Texts 5
- IV. The Title 7
- V. Burmese Enthusiasm 9
- VI. The Present Work 11

Chapter II: Mahā Maṅgala Sutta 13
- I. The Pāli Text 13
- II . Word by Word Rendering 15
- III. Translation 18

Chapter III: Notes and Comments 21
- I. The Title 21
- II. Introduction 21
- III. The Body of the Sutta 27

Chapter IV: The Highroad of Blessings 68
- I. The Thirty-eight Blessings 68
- II. General Review 70
- III. A Synthetic View 72
- IV. Our Classification 74

Chapter V: Conclusion 78

Chapter I

INTRODUCTION

I. The Glorious Sutta

Superstitions and selfish desires weave a pattern of mind which interprets objective and subjective happenings in life as forebodings of personal weal and woe. Thus, if on waking up in the morning, or on the start of a trip, or in the course of a long journey, or at the beginning of an enterprise, or during a sacred ceremony, one meets with what is taken to be a sign of good fortune, such as a flower in bloom, a smiling face, good news or even something at first sight offensive but potentially considered good, some people feel assured of success in the subsequent course of events. An auto-suggestion like this might be of some use but to place complete reliance on it, neglecting the action necessary for fulfilment and success, would be too much of wishful thinking, bound to result in frustration or failure. So much importance is attached by some people to such omens of what is supposed to be auspicious that a sort of pseudo-science has grown up playing an undesirable role in the lives of those people by choking their initiative, by sustaining their fears, by suppressing self-confidence and by the promotion of irrational attitudes in them. In the time of the Buddha such a belief was as much in evidence as today, and as he was opposed to anything that fettered the healthy growth of the human mind he raised his voice against such superstitions. He denounced "luck" or "fortune" or "auspiciousness" and proclaimed instead human behaviour, associations and activities as the real origins of "fortune" or "misfortune." Thus the emphasis was shifted from unhealthy fears and fettering superstitions to individual responsibility, rational thinking, social obligations and self-confidence. This had far-reaching effects in improving both human relationships and the efficiency of the human mind.

In Indian society in the Buddha's time (as in our own), people were addicted to superstitions about omens of good and bad luck besides being divided on their nature and implications; so it was natural that someone should inquire into the views of the Great Teacher, the Buddha, on the subject. His words of wisdom had already been an immense success not only with ordinary people but also with those in positions of power and those with great learning. A special messenger was therefore sent to meet the Buddha while he was staying at the Jetavana monastery in the garden of Anāthapiṇḍika at Sāvatthī to inquire after his views on omens.

The views expressed by the Lord in the Mahā Maṅgala Sutta are a masterpiece of practical wisdom. This Sutta was recited at the First Buddhist Council by Venerable Ānanda, the attendant of the Buddha who had memorized so many of the Buddha's discourses.

The Discourse is a charter in outline of family responsibility, social obligations, moral purification and spiritual cultivation. Within the compass of a dozen stanzas are included profound counsels and golden rules, which admirably point out the way life's journey should go if it is to reach the haven of perfect harmony, love, peace and security. Beginning with emphasis on the need for a suitable environment, the Discourse lays appropriate stress on personal discipline, righteous conduct and adequate discharge of duties towards one's near and dear ones. Then the higher virtues of humility, gratitude, patience and chastity are introduced. And step by step are reached serenity, perception of truth and Enlightenment.

A well-drawn chart like this correctly indicates the true course of progress on the stormy sea of life. Not only is the course correctly shown but also the rocks and other perils always to be found on such a journey are clearly pointed out.

The wisdom of the Mahā Maṅgala Sutta is emphasized by its spiritual appeal, which is firmly planted on this earth, while providing (or rather helping to grow) wings to soar high into the ethereal regions and beyond. The Buddha, as usual in his teachings, does not forget the needs and difficulties of the everyday world. Here lies its greatest appeal to the ordinary man, who, however much he may be fascinated by the ideal of renunciation and full-time spiritual practice, is still attached to the world through contact with family, friends and relations and the inevitable duties and obligations that this entails.

It is true to say that the appeal of the Sutta is universal. A child in school may benefit from it as may a scholar in the university. It is as much applicable to the humblest citizen as to those in power. Though proclaimed by the Buddha, it is just as valuable to non-Buddhists, valuable in fact for all peoples at all times.

Above all the Sutta is a wonderful stimulus for reform. It indicates the simple and direct way the Buddha adopted to wean people from superstitions and irrational attitudes so that they could grow and mature towards an enlightened outlook. This gradual method is unique to the Buddha. He made people see "luck," "omens" and "auspiciousness" in quite a new light, rejecting superstition and encouraging reliance upon one's own good actions. In consequence signs and omens gave way to his emphasis upon social obligations and duties founded on individual good conduct and leading to a society lighted by understanding and individual hearts enlightened by penetration of the truth.

II. Location in the Scriptures

The Mahā Maṅgala Sutta is included in that ancient anthology of the Pāli Canon called "A Collection of Discourses" (Sutta-Nipāta). This work contains a great variety of discourses, some upon basic subjects suitable for lay people, while others which have great depth are addressed to those who practise Dhamma all the time. The Sutta-Nipāta is the fifth item of the Minor Collection (Khuddaka-Nikāya) and is divided into five sections. The Mahā Maṅgala Sutta is the fourth Sutta of the second of these, called the Lesser Section. The contents of this Sutta also appear in the first item of the Minor Collection, known as the Minor Readings (Khuddaka-pāṭha), called there simply "Maṅgala Sutta."

It is interesting to note that the tenth item of the same collection, the *Jātaka* (birth stories), which has 547 chapters, each relating a previous life of the Buddha, has as the titles of the 87th and 453rd Jātakas, the Maṅgala Jātaka and the Mahā Maṅgala Jātaka respectively. These stories, though their contents are different, are interesting supplements to the Sutta because the same spirit runs through all these texts.

The following table clearly indicates the exact location in the scriptures of the Maṅgala Sutta, the Mahā Maṅgala Sutta, the Maṅgala Jātaka and the Mahā Maṅgala Jātaka.

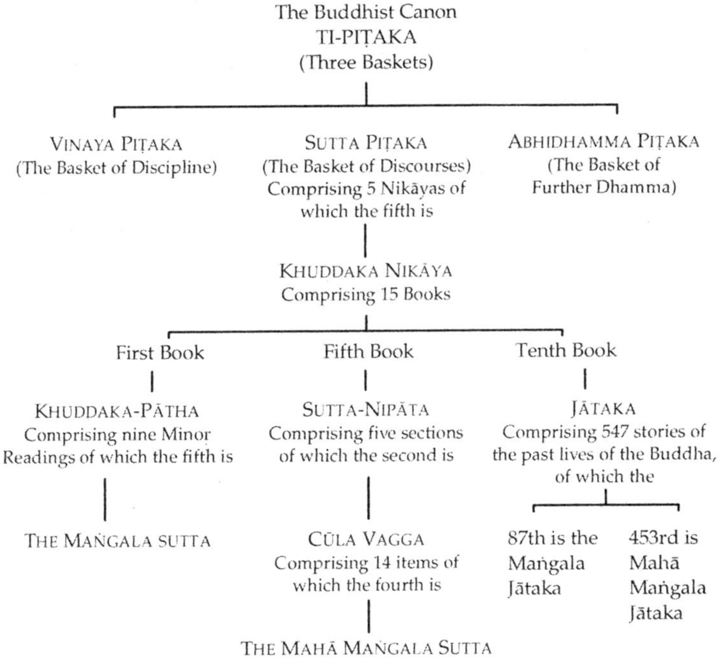

III. The Contents of These Texts

The story of the Maṅgala Jātaka concerns a brahmin said to be an expert in predictions drawn from cloth. Obsessed with the superstition that any cloth, however new or costly, once bitten by a rat was highly inauspicious (*amaṅgala*), he had a valuable garment of his thrown away into a cemetery on discovering a rat-bite on it. Hearing that the Buddha had picked up the discarded cloth, consternation seized the brahmin, as he expected ill-luck to strike down the Blessed One and those with him. He hastened to the Buddha to avert the danger before it was too late. But once in the Buddha's presence he was weaned out of his superstition and he attained insight into the Dhamma. The Buddha told him of his addiction to the same superstition in an earlier life.

The Buddha taught him the Mahā Maṅgala Jātaka about one of his previous births when he was leading the life of a hermit near Benares. He then expounded eight groups of blessings, viz. unqualified benevolence, humility, social service, liberality, domestic felicity, uprightness compelling universal respect, proper understanding of kamma-functioning and mental peace.

The above stories throw considerable light not only on the attitude of the Buddha towards superstitions, but also on the emphasis he laid on developing an enlightened outlook and virtuous life. In the Maṅgala and the Mahā Maṅgala Suttas, the latter aspect is further amplified.

We have chosen the Mahā Maṅgala Sutta as the text of the present work. It has an introduction in prose but its main body is the twelve stanzas. Each stanza has the same number of lines, and all the stanzas are in the same meter and have the same refrain. The teachings contained in these verses, since they are in agreement with other parts of the Suttas, are obviously words from the Buddha's lips. The recitation of this composition in the First Council[1] (about 543 BCE) was the work of the Venerable Ānanda, hence the words with which it opens "Thus have I heard."

IV. The Title

The title Mahā Maṅgala Sutta has three parts, namely, *mahā, maṅgala* and *sutta*. *Mahā* means "great"; used as a prefix it enlarges and emphasizes the meaning of the word or expression to which it is attached. Thus *mahādhana* (great wealth), *mahākaruṇā* (great compassion), *mahāpatha* (high road), *mahāpurisa* (great being), *mahārāja* (great king or emperor). Other examples are *mahābodhi, mahāvihāra,* etc.

The prefix *mahā* added to the title of a book or chapter adds weight and importance to the contents. The use of the prefix in this Sutta is an indication of its precious worth besides suggesting the recognition of this worth by the Arahants who compiled the Suttas in the First Council. The component *maṅgala* means an "omen," good luck, an auspice, etc. The word also signifies "auspicious ceremony," e.g. *vivāha-maṅgala* (marriage ceremony), *nāma-karaṇa-maṅgala* (name-giving ceremony). Such uses of the word are still common in India and reflect the popular and more or less superstitious ideas that the Buddha tried to supplant.

The Pāli commentators have derived the term *maṅgala* from *maṃ* (woeful condition) and *ga-la* (driving away and cutting off); therefore it means "that which is obstructive to woe". In practice it has the positive significance "conducive to weal."

---

1. This was held in the first year of the Buddhist Era, three months after the Final Nibbāna of the Great Master. No unenlightened persons sat in the Convocation, which consisted of 500 Arahants, who recited, classified and arranged the Teachings in seven months. Venerable Ānanda recited the Suttas, including of course the Mahā Maṅgala Sutta.

Maṅgala, though at times used in a spiritual sense, usually has worldly associations. It generally stands for conditions making for satisfaction, happiness and prosperity. Thus it is the most yearned-for thing in worldly happiness and domestic welfare. No wonder any sign or omen, any *maṅgala* believed to point the way to such happiness is eagerly seized upon. When it is so much of a blessing, people will eagerly seek and look for it in physical omens and material signs which they think lead to it.

Because of the differences in outlook among various people, conflicting interpretations of the omens considered auspicious are naturally found. It was to settle such differences that the Buddha was approached. But rather than condemning some viewpoints or commending certain other interpretations, he looked at the subject from a different angle and from a higher horizon, with the result that the term *maṅgala* assumed a nobler significance.

Coming to the last component of the title, originally by the term *Sutta* was meant a string or a thread. In fact the word is still used in this sense. Just as beads can be strung together by a thread into a rosary or flowers into a garland, successive arguments can be strung together into a logically brilliant whole, and sections of a story or a sermon can be threaded together to present a good way to practice. The symbolic use of the word "*sutta*" to mean a discourse is this "threading together."

In English, too, the word "thread" has been the symbol of continuity as suggested by the phrase "a thread of thought." As progressive continuity is obvious in a series of logically connected ideas and events in a narrative, it is symbolized by a thread or a *sutta*. Evidently a knot in the thread represents "a concentrated deep idea" inviting focused attention for its unravelling. Such reflections result in flashes of wisdom and inspiration.

It was in this sense that the thinkers and sages in ancient India used the term "*sutta*"; also it was in this form that they expressed their thoughts.

The Discourse on the Highest Blessings is truly a "*sutta*," a threaded collection of gems of the highest blessings in life, blessings varied in nature and scope according to the needs of the individual in different stages on life's journey. The Sutta really is a sublime garland of blessings full of fragrance, radiant with benevolence, shining with truth and aglow with practical utility.

V. Burmese Enthusiasm

The Mahā Maṅgala Sutta by itself, or as part of the Sutta-Nipāta or of the Khuddakapāṭha or as a part of some compilations, is available in several editions in the Sinhalese, Thai and Burmese scripts, with or without translations and commentaries in those languages.

The Sutta has a special significance in the national life of Burma. It is certainly Burma's most valuable heritage of proven truth. The Sutta is one of the first lessons a child in Burma learns by heart. Memorizing it eagerly, he recites and untiringly repeats its stanzas naturally with gusto till their constituents seem to vibrate his entire being. And what is more marvellous is that the effect is life-long. Even in rash youth and old age, the chanting of the Sutta coming from the precincts of a monastery or classroom recalls memories of childhood and the need for self-cultivation to direct one's steps towards those actions which lead to peace in one's own heart and happiness for others. Today throughout the length and breadth of the country children and adults are schooled in the Maṅgala Sutta.

There are dozens of admirable books and booklets on the Maṅgala Sutta available in Burmese. Most of these are recent works and very well written in a way to convey the practical message straight to the heart. Of the older works, *Maṅgalatthadīpani,*[2] a voluminous book of over 760 pages written by Maṅgalabon-gyaw Sayādaw at the court of Amarapura in 1854. This is not only an impressive piece of classical literature but also an abundant storehouse of well-told stories illustrating moral, practical and spiritual values in the Sutta. The method is commendable because of its proven value making the listeners and readers understand vividly the practical import of the Sutta's teachings. It is good to see that even the latest works freely draw upon this old method. Thus modern Burmese authors, while imparting a fresh touch to their writings, are wise in not losing hold of the treasure-store of the past. In the present work, unfortunately, the illustrative stories cannot find a place, because they would greatly increase its length.

---

2. This must be a similar work to the Pāli language book of the same name which is widely studied in Thailand. It was written by Phra Sirimaṅgalācariya Thera of Chiengmai (northern Siam) and completed in 1528.

VI. The Present Work

There have been many translations of this Sutta, some with the Pāli, some without, and it is not possible or necessary to list them here. That there are so many is an eloquent testimony to the popularity of the Sutta. In spite of this great appreciation, the author does not know any works in English exclusively devoted to the Sutta apart from one publication[3] and some leaflets. Considering the value, importance and popularity of this precious Sutta, the need for more and detailed works is obvious. Therefore, it seems there is no need for an apology in offering this book to the reader.

The plan of the present work is simple: the Mahā Maṅgala Sutta is presented first in original Pāli together with a word-by-word English rendering of it and a more literal translation. Then follow notes and comments explaining the contents. However, all the issues do not require exhaustive treatment. While it has been found necessary to deal thoroughly with certain subjects of special Buddhist interest or of a complicated nature, others easily intelligible and needing no comments are barely mentioned. In the last chapter the Blessings are classified.

It was the author's desire to give a living Burmese touch to this work by assigning a chapter to a captivating contemporary popular song in Burmese on the Sutta but the difficulties encountered in rendering this into English proved insurmountable; so the attempt had to be given up.

---

3. *Maṅgalasutta Vaṇṇanā* by K. Gunaratana Thera, Penang 1952.

In the preparation of this book the valuable assistance received from the Venerable Nyanatiloka's *Buddhist Dictionary*[4] is gratefully acknowledged. The author is also thankful to U Ba Thin and other friends who read the Burmese text to him.

4. Buddhist Publication Society, Kandy.

Chapter II

Mahā Maṅgala Sutta

I. The Pāli Text

Evaṃ me sutaṃ. Ekaṃ samayaṃ Bhagavā Sāvatthiyaṃ viharati Jetavane Anāthapiṇḍikassa ārāme. Atha kho aññatarā devatā abhikkantāya rattiyā abhikkantavaṇṇā kevalakappaṃ Jetavanaṃ obhāsetvā yena Bhagavā tena upasaṅkami, upasaṅkamitvā Bhagavantaṃ abhivādetvā ekamantaṃ aṭṭhāsi. Ekamantaṃ ṭhitā kho sā devatā Bhagavantaṃ gāthāya ajjhabhāsi:

I

Bahū devā manussā ca, maṅgalāni acintayuṃ
ākaṅkhamānā sotthānaṃ, brūhi maṅgalam-uttamaṃ.

II

Asevanā ca bālānaṃ, paṇḍitānañ ca sevanā
pūjā ca pūjanīyānaṃ, etam maṅgalam-uttamaṃ.

III

Patirūpadesavāso ca, pubbe ca kata-puññatā
attasammāpaṇidhi ca, etam maṅgalam-uttamaṃ.

IV

Bahusaccañ ca sippañ ca, vinayo ca susikkhito
subhāsitā ca yā vācā, etam maṅgalam-uttamaṃ.

V

Mātā-pitu upaṭṭhānaṃ, putta-dārassa saṅgaho
anākulā ca kammantā, etam maṅgalam-uttamaṃ.

VI

Dānañ ca dhammacariyā ca, ñātakānañ ca saṅgaho
anavajjāni kammāni, etam maṅgalam-uttamaṃ.

VII

Āratī viratī pāpā, majjapānā ca saññamo
appamādo ca dhammesu, etam maṅgalam-uttamaṃ.

VIII

Gāravo ca nivāto ca, santuṭṭhī ca kataññutā
kālena dhammasavanaṃ, etam maṅgalam-uttamaṃ.

IX

Khantī ca sovacassatā, samaṇānañ ca dassanaṃ
kālena dhammasākacchā, etam maṅgalam-uttamaṃ.

X

Tapo ca brahmacariyañ-ca, ariyasaccāna-dassanaṃ
nibbāna-sacchikiriyā ca etam maṅgalam-uttamaṃ.

XI

Phuṭṭhassa lokadhammehi, cittaṃ yassa na kampati
asokaṃ virajaṃ khemaṃ, etam maṅgalam-uttamaṃ.

XII

Etādisāni katvāna, sabbattham-aparājitā
sabbattha sotthiṃ gacchanti, taṃ tesaṃ maṅgalam-uttamaṃ.

(*Mahāmaṅgalasuttaṃ niṭṭhitaṃ*)

II . Word by Word Rendering

Evaṃ (thus) *me* (I) *sutaṃ* (heard):

Ekaṃ (one) *samayaṃ* (time) *Bhagavā* (the Blessed One, the Buddha) *Sāvatthiyaṃ* (near Sāvatthī) *viharati* (was staying) *Jetavane* (in the Jeta Grove) *Anāthapiṇḍikassa ārāme* (in Anāthapiṇḍika's monastery). *Atha kho* (certainly then) *aññatarā* (a certain) *devatā* (deity, a *deva*) *abhikkantāya* (towards, far advanced) *rattiyā* (night) *abhikkantavaṇṇā* (of surpassing brilliance and beauty) *kevalakappaṃ* (the entire) *Jetavanaṃ* (Jeta Grove) *obhāsetvā* (having illumined) *yena Bhagavā* (where the Blessed One was) *tena upasaṅkami* (approached that place) *upasaṅkamitvā* (having reached) *Bhagavantaṃ abhivādetvā* (having offered profound salutations to the Blessed One) *ekamantaṃ* (aside) *aṭṭhāsi* (stood). *Ekamantaṃ ṭhitā kho* (having stood aside) *sā devatā* (the deity) *Bhagavantaṃ* (to the Blessed One) *gāthāya* (in verse) *ajjhabhāsi* (addressed respectfully).

I

Bahū (many) *devā* (deities) *manussā ca* (and human beings) *maṅgalāni* (over blessings) *acintayuṃ* (have pondered), *ākaṅkhamānā* (hoping for) *sotthānaṃ* (safety) *brūhi* (please expound) *maṅgalam-uttamaṃ* (the Highest Blessing).

II

Asevanā (not to associate with) *ca bālānaṃ* (the foolish people) *paṇḍitānañ ca* (and the wise) *sevanā* (to associate with) *pūjā ca* (homage) *pūjanīyānaṃ* (those worthy of homage) *etam* (this) *maṅgalam-uttamaṃ* (the Highest Blessing).

III

Paṭirūpa (congenial) *desa* (locality) *vāso* (for residence) *ca* (and) *pubbe ca* (in the past) *kata-puññatā* (having made merit) *atta* (one's self) *sammā* (rightly) *paṇidhi ca* (directed) *etam maṅgalam-uttamaṃ* (this, the Highest Blessing).

IV

Bahu (ample) *saccañ* (learning) *ca sippañ* (and proficiency in crafts) *ca* (and) *vinayo ca* (moral discipline) *susikkhito* (well trained) *subhāsitā ca* (and well spoken) *yā vācā* (words) *etam maṅgalam-uttamaṃ* (this, the Highest Blessing).

V

Mātā-pitu (mother and father) *upaṭṭhānaṃ* (to support) *putta-dārassa* (children and wife) *saṅgaho* (to cherish) *anākulā ca* (and unconflicting) *kammantā* (types of work) *etam maṅgalam-uttamaṃ* (this, the Highest Blessing).

VI

Dānañ (giving) *ca dhammacariyā* (living by Dhamma) *ca* (and) *ñātakānañ* (relatives) *ca saṅgaho* (supporting) *anavajjāni* (blameless) *kammāni* (actions) *etam maṅgalam-uttamaṃ* (this, the Highest Blessing).

VII

Āratī (avoidance) *viratī* (abstinence) *pāpā* (from evil) *majjapānā ca* (intoxicating drinks) *saññamo* (to refrain from) *appamādo ca* (and diligence in) *dhammesu* (acts of virtue) *etam maṅgalam-uttamaṃ* (this, the Highest Blessing).

VIII

Gāravo (reverence) *ca* (and) *nivāto* (humility) *ca* (and) *santuṭṭhī* (contentment) *ca kataññutā* (and gratitude) *kālena* (timely) *dhammasavanaṃ* (hearing Dhamma) *etam maṅgalam-uttamaṃ* (this, the Highest Blessing).

IX

Khantī (patience) *ca sovacassatā* (and amenability to correction) *samaṇānañ ca* (of monk) *dassanaṃ* (seeing) *kālena* (timely) *dhammasākacchā* (discussions on the Dhamma) *etam maṅgalam-uttamaṃ* (this, the Highest Blessing).

X

Tapo (energetic restraint) *ca brahmacariyāñ-ca* (and holy and chaste life) *ariyassaccāna*-(and the Noble Truths) *dassanaṃ* (seeing) *nibbāna-sacchikiriyā ca* (and realization of Nibbāna) *etam maṅgalam-uttamaṃ* (this, the Highest Blessing).

XI

Phuṭṭhassa (touched by) *lokadhammehi* (worldly conditions) *cittaṃ yassa* (whose mind) *na kampati* (is not shaken) *asokaṃ* (free from sorrow) *virajaṃ* (free from passion) *khemaṃ* (secure) *etam maṅgalam-uttamaṃ* (this, the Highest Blessing).

XII

Etādisāni (these things) *katvāna* (having fulfilled) *sabbattham-* (everywhere) *aparājitā* (unvanquished) *sabbattha* (everywhere) *sotthiṃ* (in happiness and safety) *gacchanti* (they go) *taṃ* (that) *tesaṃ* (to them) *maṅgalam-uttamaṃ* (the Highest Blessing).

Mahāmaṅgalasuttaṃ (The Discourse on Great Blessings) *niṭṭhitaṃ* (is ended).

III. Translation

Thus have I heard:

Once while the Blessed One was staying in the vicinity of Sāvatthī, in the Jeta Grove, in Anāthapiṇḍika's monastery, a certain deity, whose surpassing brilliance and beauty illumined the entire Jeta Grove, late one night came to the presence of the Blessed One; having come to him and offered profound salutations he stood on one side and spoke to him reverently in the following verse:

I

Many deities and human beings
Have pondered what are blessings,
Which they hope will bring them safety.
Declare to them, Sir, the Highest Blessing.

(To this the Blessed One replied):

II

With fools no company keeping,
With the wise ever consorting,
To the worthy homage paying:
This, the Highest Blessing.

III

Congenial place to dwell,
In the past merits making,
One's self directed well:
This, the Highest Blessing.

IV

Ample learning, in crafts ability,
With a well-trained disciplining,
Well-spoken words, civility:
This, the Highest Blessing.

V

Mother, father well supporting,
Wife and children duly cherishing,
Types of work unconflicting:
This, the Highest Blessing.

VI

Acts of giving, righteous living,
Relatives and kin supporting,
Actions blameless then pursuing:
This, the Highest Blessing.

VII

Avoiding evil and abstaining,
From besotting drinks refraining,
Diligence in Dhamma doing:
This, the Highest Blessing.

VIII

Right reverence and humility,
Contentment and a grateful bearing,
Hearing Dhamma when it's timely:
This, the Highest Blessing.

IX

Patience, meekness when corrected,
Seeing monks and then discussing

The Dhamma when it's timely:
This, the Highest Blessing.

X

Self-restraint and holy life,
Seeing the Noble Truths,
Realization of Nibbāna:
This, the Highest Blessing.

XI

Though touched by worldly circumstances,
Never his mind is wavering,
Sorrowless, stainless and secure:
This, the Highest Blessing.

XII

Since by acting in this way,
They are everywhere unvanquished,
And everywhere they go in safety:
Theirs, the Highest Blessings.

Here ends the Discourse on Great Blessings.

CHAPTER III

NOTES AND COMMENTS

I. The Title

Mahā Maṅgala Sutta:

Discourse on the Highest Blessings, the real omens, or the most auspicious and "lucky" actions.

II. Introduction

(A) *Evaṃ me sutaṃ*

The Discourses and Suttas of the Buddhist scriptures begin with these words. The history behind this short sentence is as follows. Some three months after the final Nibbāna of the Buddha, when King Ajātasattu had been on the throne already for about eight years, the First Great Council was held under royal patronage at the Sattapaṇṇi Cave in Rājagaha, the capital, where five hundred Arahants assembled to recite, classify and group together the Teachings of the Master. Venerable Mahā Kassapa presided, while the Venerables Upāli and Ānanda rehearsed the Vinaya (monastic discipline) and the Suttas or discourses respectively. The Council finished its work after seven months, during which time they arranged the entire Teachings of the Master, that is, the collections of the Vinaya rules and the Suttas.

To the Venerable Ānanda, as he was most learned in the Master's discourses, fell the arduous task of rehearsing the Suttas in the Great Council. He prefixed each discourse with the expression *"Evaṃ me suttaṃ"* ("Thus have I heard"), thus personally testifying to the authenticity of the Suttas. At that time religious teachings generally were committed to memory, so the Buddha's Teachings too were presented at first in this way. Venerable Ānanda's words, "Thus have I heard," were prefixed to the memorized version, which thereafter was passed down from teacher to pupil by oral tradition until it was committed to writing for the first time at Aluvihārā in the central province of Sri Lanka (about 80 BCE in the reign and under the patronage of King Vaṭṭagāmaṇi Abhaya.

The Council was held at the capital of Anurādhapura with its conclusion, the writing down of the Suttas, Vinaya and Abhidhamma, at Aluvihāra. The Council was necessary for safeguarding the texts from loss through invasions, famines and the whims of kings; also from serious alterations and interpolations by unscrupulous people. There is a legend that the Ti-piṭaka was inscribed on gold sheets which were said to have been deposited in the rocks at Aluvihāra. Considering the amount of gold which would be needed, this seems very unlikely, though some condensed passages may have been inscribed in this way and enshrined.

As the Venerable Ānanda was a stream-winner[5] who had seen Dhamma himself, as well as being a devoted attendant of the Buddha, his words "Thus have

---

5. This refers to the time when he listened to the Buddha's discourses. He attained Arahantship immediately before the commencement of the First Council (BPS Ed.).

I heard" prefixed to the Mahā Maṅgala Sutta, as to most other Suttas, invest these texts with the seal of authenticity.

(B) *Bhagavā*

As one of the epithets of the Buddha, it occurs frequently in the scriptures meaning "having good luck" i.e. auspicious, fortunate. It is generally translated as "the Blessed One" or "the Exalted One," though the full meaning of 'One who apportions' (the Dhamma) with the knowledge of what is exactly suitable to them, cannot be conveyed in English. The usual formula of homage also has this epithet at the beginning: "*Namo tassa Bhagavato Arahato Sammāsambuddhassa*" meaning "Homage to the Blessed One, the Liberated One, the Fully Enlightened One." There are many other titles by which the Buddha is known such as *Tilokanātha* (Lord of the Three Worlds), *Dhammarāja* (the Lord of Truth), *Tathāgata* (lit. Thus Gone; but more fully meaning, "Gone" in the same way of Enlightenment and Nibbāna as Buddhas in the past), *Sugata* (the Happy One), *Sakyamuni* (the Sākyan Sage), and *Sākyasīha* (the Sākyan Lion) and so on. The term "Buddha" itself is not a name but means "the Enlightened One," "the Awakened One," which signifies the zenith of perfection, supreme and final release from all types of existence or being, and the actual attainment of Nibbāna during life. (See also Stanza X on Nibbāna.)

(C) *Sāvatthi, Jetavana, Anāthapiṇḍika*

Sāvatthī (Sk. Srāvastī) was an ancient city which is identified with the village of Sahet-mahet in the present-day Indian state of Uttar Pradesh. It was the capital of the powerful kingdom of Kosala in the sixth century BCE. The great merchant and benefactor Anāthapiṇḍika, whose real name was Sudatta, bought Prince Jeta's pleasure grove in this city for a fabulous price (said to be as much as eighteen crores of gold coins) and built a monastery which he presented to the Buddha. The monastery was called Anāthapiṇḍika Ārāma and the grove was known as Jetavana, Prince Jeta's Grove. Here the Buddha stayed for twenty-four rainy seasons and gave many important discourses. The Mahā Maṅgala Sutta is one of them.

(D) *Devatā*

In Buddhist teachings there are six realms of celestial beings (*devaloka*) superior to the human world, which together comprise the "happy states" in the world of sensual desire or *kāmaloka*. These beings are of greater or lesser splendour and brilliance and they live very long lives enjoying the happy fruits of their past good kamma. On the expiry of this, however, they gravitate to a rebirth in accordance with their residual merit, for the Devas make little new good kamma and can be compared to rich people living on their capital, which will run out sooner or later. And their new rebirth is not necessarily a better one; it may well be worse and even below the human state.

Though short-lived and having a coarse body, man is in a way superior to these celestials, as he can increase his merits by further wholesome actions and can even attain the highest goal, Nibbāna. That is why even celestial beings look to the Buddha for guidance and to Noble Ones for assistance.

At the time when the Buddha was teaching in India, it is said that not only human beings were divided about what was an omen, what was lucky or auspicious and what were really blessings, but also celestials were confused on the subject. As no one could decide this matter, an assembly of celestials deputed one of their number to visit the Buddha to get his views to clarify their doubts.

There are many stories of heavenly messengers visiting the Buddha. They usually visited him late at night, as the accounts say, "when the night was far spent," or just before dawn. Sometimes they visited him in human form and at other times they went in celestial form. Sometimes the designation "*devatā*" is even used for forest-dwelling spirits who also visited the Buddha. In this particular case it was a radiant being from a celestial abode whose presence filled the entire grove with splendour, turning the darkest hour of night into more than the brilliance of day. Materialists may consider such a being to be imagination but there are people with personal experience of such forms of existence.

These heavens have other states superior to them, two more spheres, namely, the world of subtle form (*rūpaloka*) and the formless world (*arūpaloka*). The former have sixteen realms while in the latter the inhabitants are super-celestial and even longer lived, their life span running into thousands of aeons.

Still, they are also subject to change. These celestial and super-celestial regions together with the human realms and the four sub-human planes or the evil states (*duggati*), in all totalling thrty-one planes of existence, comprise the range of phenomenal existence termed *saṃsāra*, literally the "wandering on".[6] The inhabitants of these planes, whether human or sub-human, celestial or super-celestial, are all alike in this: their existences depend on the different types of good and bad kamma made by them. They are alike too in that all are subject to the same law of impermanence (*anicca*), suffering (*dukkha*) and not-self (*anattā*), the difference being in the quality of their lives, with more or less of happiness and suffering, opportunities for development or lack of them. These are the fruits of kamma made in past and present lives. All these beings, high and low, are bound (by themselves) to the incessantly moving wheel of saṃsāra. If there were no way out, each individual would go on forever because of intoxication with greed (*lobha*), hatred (*dosa*) and delusion (*moha*) and so suffering here, suffering there and suffering everywhere—it would have no end. The way beyond what is marked by impermanence, suffering and non-self was pointed out by the Buddha, who, after his supreme awakening to truth, showed the path which leads to the final release of Nibbāna.

Birth as a human being is best according to the Buddha's teachings, for in spite of his frailties, man has adequate personal and environmental conditions for scaling spiritual heights, while he may have seen enough suffering to goad him on. Thus each human being has the potential to become an Arahant or a Buddha; though not everyone, of course, has golden chances and magnificent opportunities, still all are capable of raising themselves to some extent, and some to heights far above the range of even the highest gods. It depends on how each person avails oneself of the opportunities. One should always

---

6. See Ledi Sayādaw, *The Noble Eightfold Path and Its Factors Explained*, Wheel Publication No. 245/247, for a diagram illustrating this.

make the greatest effort to turn one's footsteps towards a good heavenly birth or towards Nibbāna, the highest goal; otherwise evil kamma may rivet chains which drag one down to sufferings or even into fires of the hells. The Buddha shows the way: the pilgrim has to walk that way himself.

The Buddha is called the "Light of the Three Worlds" and any of their inhabitants, even the gods, may approach him for everyday guidance or spiritual instruction. Usually people go to the gods (or to one of them, God) for guidance, but it is the various gods who came to the Buddha with their problems. In this way we can understand the significance of the god's visit mentioned in the Mahā Maṅgala Sutta.

III. The Body of the Sutta

Stanza I: *Many deities and human beings ...*

Here a question is asked to which the subsequent eleven stanzas provide the answer. The question is put by a deva, the accredited spokesman of the deva-world. The deva presents to the Buddha not only the contentions about "blessings" prevalent in the heavens but also those in the human world, thus covering the seven happy planes (*sugati*) of the sensual world (*kāmaloka*), and perhaps more.

The points mentioned or implied are:

1. That the inhabitants of the deva and human worlds desired happiness and safety, which were connected, they thought, with what they considered "auspicious" or "lucky."

2. That many of them had been deeply pondering for a long time what were real blessings, omens or auspices.
3. That their reflection was rooted in a strong desire for personal welfare, safety and subjective happiness.
4. That in spite of their sincere and persistent efforts, they could not agree regarding the real nature of *maṅgalam-uttamaṃ*, the Highest Blessings.
5. That only the Buddha, the embodiment of Supreme Wisdom, could throw proper light on the subject.
6. That, therefore, the deva approached the Buddha with the question troubling the human and deva worlds.
7. That the Blessed One was earnestly implored to clearly expound the truth on the subject, for the welfare of gods and men.

From the above, two distinct issues emerge:

1. That happiness in the human and deva worlds leaves much to be desired.
2. That the inhabitants of these planes have an intense desire to attain perfection of happiness.

In the world of sensual desire, happiness is conditioned by subjective desire, efficiency of the senses and the existence of suitable objects. As all these are subject to incessant change, the consequent happiness of the senses is transient (cf. *sabbe kāmā aniccā*, "all sensual pleasures are impermanent") and therefore lacks lasting satisfaction. Sensual *gratification* is in fact a deception, though if it is understood, this may lead to the path of deliverance. This is the *escape* from sense-desires. But when gratification is not understood, it may intensify desire for sense pleasures, with dissatisfaction, regret or sorrow, which are the *danger* in them, following sooner or later. The Buddha has many times spoken about sense-desire, gratification, danger and escape.

With these clear facts, one must draw the following conclusions:

1. That in the human and deva worlds, beings desire to perfect their happiness.
2. That their happiness, when it is rooted in desire for sensual gratification, can never reach perfection.

So happiness in the world of sensual desire is, at best, only relative and therefore subject to constant change.

The Buddha immediately realized both the relative and the supra-mundane importance of this question concerning the acts of blessedness or true omens. He gave a reply in which both these aspects were thoroughly considered. By re-interpretation the Buddha boldly by-passed the superstitious meaning of the word "*maṅgala,*" looking at auspiciousness from the practical viewpoint. Beginning his answer in a very down-to-earth way, he gradually described, in a steadily rising scale, blessings or omens leading higher and higher, finally to the supra-mundane state of Nibbāna.

Stanza II: *With fools no company keeping …*

Sevanā and *asevanā* literally mean "service" and the "absence of service." Applied to the nouns "wise men" (*paṇḍita*) and "fools" (*bālā*), the meaning is "association" or "non-association"; thus we get "not associating with fools" and "associating with the wise." The underlying idea is that one must not follow after fools or take them as a standard for conduct or personal guidance, but follow the wise. One waxes or wanes in good qualities according to with whom one associates.

Paṇḍitā[7] means the wise, learned, experienced and those capable of giving advice which is practical and wholesome.

Bālā originally meant "children," and hence weak persons and then foolish and stupid people, the opposite of the wise, people with minds undeveloped, those whose behaviour is coarse and rough, trouble-makers who tend to give advice which is unwholesome and evil. They lack discrimination and a sense of judgment, and are heedless of Dhamma, reckless in action and regardless of the consequences. These people are undesirable company. This interpretation of *bāla* does not include children who, are on the whole good and graceful.

The emphasis is on keeping away from and not getting entangled with people who, though grown up in years, have none of the graces of children but all their failings and shortcomings; these are the people possessing the characteristics of "fools." Their company can only harm. They certainly are very unfortunate, but association with them is not auspicious and their mental and emotional constitution is such that they do not profit from beneficial guidance. Far from gaining anything themselves, they will rather drag even a good man into trouble and danger. The example usually given from the Suttas is that of the Buddha's cousin Devadatta dragging King Ajātasattu to hell by instigating him to kill his father who was a virtuous king.

---

7. For details see the Dhammapada verses of the chapters on Fools, *Bālavaggo,* and Wise, *Paṇḍitavaggo.*

The Suttas warn one against companionship with bad people in this way: because of bad company one gives ear to evil advice; because of such advice evil reflections occupy the mind; because of such reflections mental confusion prevails and the senses are uncontrolled; as a result of this, actions of body and speech are faulty and the five hindrances[8] gain strength holding one to sensual cravings and resulting in sufferings.

On the other hand, through companionship with the wise the sequence is: listening to good advice, rational faith, noble thoughts, clear thinking, self-control, good conduct, conquest of the hindrances, gaining of wisdom and the consequent liberation.

It should be said here that while it is essential for an ordinary person to keep away from bad company, one who is advanced in self-control, full of loving-kindness and compassion and thus immune to the evils of such association may live in the midst of such persons for the noble purpose of leading them to a better understanding while all the time on guard against evil influences. Though his body moves with them, his mind should be beyond their influence. If he is not certain of his own self-control, he should avoid the company of such people. He may associate with them only when he is sure that his good influence is flowing to them, and not their evil influence to him. The advice of the Buddha is that there should not be any

---

8. These are five obstacles blinding mental vision, viz. lustful desire (*kāmacchanda*), ill-will (*vyāpāda*), lethargy and drowsiness (*thīna-middha*), agitation and worry (*uddhacca-kukkucca*) and sceptical doubt (*vicikicchā*). When these are present in the mind, discrimination, judgment and action become faulty.

entanglement with fools, from which one can neither extricate oneself nor them.

Pūjā and *pūjanīyānaṃ* mean "homage" and "those worthy of homage." The examples are the Buddha, monks (*bhikkhus*), holy persons, parents, teachers—all of whom are of great assistance to us in life.

Some people do not like to show respect, or to express reverence, even when it is quite proper to do so in the presence of those who have greater and purer conduct in mind, speech and body, than they have. Such people suffer from pride, they estimate themselves too highly and do not want to admit that others could have achieved more than themselves. They are, so to speak, "standing in their own light" and they will not be able to see the right way to go. Their pride will only lead them to the strengthening of other defilements of mind, and so they go from bad to worse. They have shut the door in their own faces and can go no further. And how they quarrel with others!

Respectful persons are not like this. They are a pleasure to live and associate with, unlike people with much pride. They not only "fit" well into whatever society they are in, they also have the ability to learn more since they recognize that others know more than they do. So they have one of the factors necessary for any progress, whether in worldly prosperity or on the Path of Dhamma. We shall see later that humility is another "Blessing." This practice of honouring the honourable is the foundation for humility.

Stanza III: *Congenial place to dwell ...*

Patirūpa-desa-vāso means "residence in a suitable and pleasant locality." For life to be pleasant, the dwelling place must be comfortable, secure in construction, tidy and clean in appearance, properly maintained, and besides it is helpful if it is in a good neighbourhood and inhabited by agreeable people. The commentators amplify the meaning by explaining that a suitable locality should have in it people who practise the Noble Dhamma, the evidence of this being the existence of shrines, monks and monasteries and many good people engaged in meritorious deeds.

Residence in a place inhabited by quarrelsome and trouble-making citizens, where one is bossed about by a dictatorial and corrupt government, where the climate is inimical with frequent ravages by floods, famines, earthquakes and epidemics, where the air is charged with hatred and mutual suspicion, and where freedom of thought and action is reduced to a minimum; in brief, residence in a place having many factors and conditions obstructive to the practice of Dhamma and not conducive to physical, moral and spiritual well-being, is just the opposite of what is meant by a suitable environment.

When selection of a place for residence is considered, a Buddhist bears in mind the advantage of being near a source of Dhamma, besides, of course, more mundane advantages such as nearness to his work place.

Pubbe ca kata-puññatā: "merit made in the past." Obviously it is a blessing to have done meritorious deeds in the past. A Buddhist, unlike others who take existence as beginning with birth in this life, understands the range covered by the term "*pubbe*" (the past) to comprise a vast chain of existences, each life preceded by an earlier one in an unbroken and unlimited succession. The Buddha has said that the beginning of the round of birth and death is inconceivable, for beings are blinded by ignorance and impelled by their cravings to make more and more kamma, which means the experience of more and more lives.

Action is performed by one's body (*kāya-kamma*) or by speech (*vacī-kamma*) or by mind (*mano-kamma*). These actions are called kamma when will, intention or volition is involved in the performance of "action." If there were no "will" involved, there would be no results or fruits of kamma. Throughout life one goes on making kamma and experiencing the results: some kamma bears immediate results, some are delayed in result, whereas another fails to fruit because suitable conditions for this to occur are not found. At death the continuity of the potential results of kamma (*kamma-vipāka*) in the stream of mind—which includes feeling (*vedanā*), perception (*saññā*), mental formations (*saṅkhārā*) and consciousness (*viññāṇa*)—are the only real traces of the individual, his body (*rūpa*) having suffered disintegration. These potential results of kamma must ripen, and the only way that this can happen is through rebirth.

This means the attraction of the mental continuity to a suitable couple who are having sexual intercourse and where conception is possible. This applies among human beings and animals where reproduction involves sexual union. With other kinds of kamma governing the place of birth, existence begins spontaneously without parents, as among all the gods and among all types of sub-human birth with the exception of animals. Where one is born depends generally upon the quality of the past kamma which is ready to ripen, more specifically it depends upon the last thought in the mind of the dying person.

In the new existence, that individual will experience the fruits of some of the past kamma, while if born as a human being he will make more new kamma to add to the store of potential results. At the end of that new term of life what remains of the individual is again his mental continuity containing his potential results of kamma, and it is this which again determines and conditions his next existence. Thus the cycle goes on, death followed by birth, birth by death, and so on.

The final release from this ocean of "death-birth-death" comes only for a Buddha or Arahant whose body is worn out, who has broken the pattern of making kamma and has no potential result to experience. Such a person is freed from the rounds of suffering, incessant change and selfhood, to know and see for himself or herself the highest goal, Nibbāna.

As kamma is varied in nature, so are its results. Kamma may be unwholesome (*akusala-kamma*) or wholesome (*kusala-kamma*), the former being rooted in greed (*lobha*), hatred (*dosa*) or delusion (*moha*), while the latter has its roots in generosity (literally, greedlessness, *alobha*), loving-kindness (*adosa* or hatelessness) or wisdom (literally, undeludedness, *amoha*). Wholesome kamma made with these last three roots is also known as merit—those actions which cleanse and purify the mind of the doer.

Each person makes wholesome and unwholesome kamma as well as having a store of resultants from past kamma, some actual and bearing fruit while others are potential, so the ingredients vary with each person. "Whatever kamma a person performs, good or evil, he will be the heir to it," says the Buddha. Thus the influence of past lives of an individual on his present experience can be more or less strong. If he tormented other beings, he may suffer with a disease; if he was habitually angry, he inherits ugliness; while stinginess gives him the heritage of poverty, indolence of illiteracy; envy in the past a low position in this one and so on. On the other hand, from wholesome actions one inherits health, beauty, wealth, wisdom, noble birth and so on. Truly it is a blessing to have done good deeds in the past! There is no inheritance better than that resulting from good kamma: to be an heir to such an inheritance means that one starts life with an excellent advantage. It is for this reason that the Buddha praised "the merit garnered in the past" and declared it a blessing in this life.

Attasammāpaṇidhi: "one's self rightly directed." This means one must decide on a proper objective in life and set oneself on the right path leading to it.

The emphasis is on "one's own self": one should try to direct oneself to the desired goal by the efforts one makes.[9] This encourages self-confidence and discourages dependence upon the grace of gods or men. Many people pass their lives in the wrong course, engaged in evil practices of the body, speech and mind. Such people, perhaps we are among them, should cherish right desires and open a new and wholesome direction for their lives. Others, who already consider themselves to have a wholesome way of living, should review their situation from time to time not only to avoid lapses but also to progress further in the right direction.

---

9. What about concern for others? This is just the initial stage of practice when one must be concerned with one's own good conduct. Later, having developed in Dhamma, one can manifest compassion for other people.

We can understand clearly what is meant by rightly directing oneself, in this comment: The unvirtuous person establishes himself in virtue (the five precepts for instance); the faithless person establishes himself in excellent faith; the avaricious person establishes himself in generosity. Along these lines everyone has something to do.

Stanza IV: *Ample learning, in crafts ability …*

Bahusaccañ ca sippañ ca: "ample learning and proficiency in crafts."

Bahusaccaṃ is read by some as *bahussutaṃ*, which means "great learning through hearing." In the time of the Buddha, education was mostly through oral tradition, written knowledge not being very common. Consequently one was considered learned according to what one had memorized after having heard learned people talk. This standard of erudition applied particularly to religious learning. Obviously a pupil needed certain abilities such as a good memory, keen desire to learn and to associate with the learned, also a capacity to understand their teachings. Thus *bahusaccaṃ* means "much learning through direct contact with the learned." This is a blessing whether the knowledge gained is used for Dhamma-practice or, restrained by moral conduct, for one's livelihood.

Bahu-sippaṃ means "proficiency in some art or handicraft," which implies "practical knowledge of some art, science or handicraft." We understand that the Buddha saw skill in some art or craft as a blessing too. Not only knowledge is praised by him but also manual work wherever this is not tainted by unwholesome actions. One's "craft" should therefore be in accordance with the precepts when it may be used either for hobby or livelihood. Among Bhikkhus too there are "crafts" which it is good to be skilled in—such as making robes—and such skills are a blessing for one's fellow monks.

Vinayo ca susikkhito: "well-learned discipline."

For one who leads the householder's life this means abstaining from the ten courses of unwholesome action.

The ten that should be abstained from so that one makes no evil kamma are:

1. kamma by way of body: killing living beings, taking what is not given, wrong conduct in sexual desires,
2. kamma by way of speech: false speech, malicious speech, harsh speech, gossip,
3. kamma by way of mind: covetousness, ill will and wrong views.

A layman who disciplines himself in these ten is rightly called an excellent person. People like this are sure to make further gains on the path whenever they make efforts. (See also "practice of Dhamma" under stanza VI.)

The moral discipline in the case of a monk is stricter than for a householder; he must train himself not to fall into the various classes of offences laid down by the Buddha.

Subhāsitā ca yā vācā: "well-spoken words, civility."

By this, one would usually understand speech which is devoid of the four defects, as given in the list under "well-trained discipline." And certainly what one speaks and how one speaks it are very important, considering all the words which pour out of our mouths every day. However, the commentary says that "well-spoken words" consist of words used while teaching Dhamma to other people. This must be true, for Dhamma is always for one's benefit though of course much depends on how it is taught. Dhamma words can never be ill-spoken words, since they

1. are true,
2. bring concord,
3. are compassionate,
4. and meaningful.

In this way they are a blessing both to the speaker and to the listener.

Stanza V: *"Mother, father well supporting ..."*

Mātā-pitu upaṭṭhānaṃ means adequately supporting, looking after properly, waiting on patiently and rendering proper service to mother and father.

People these days do not always look after their parents. In western lands they often prefer to get some institution to take care of them as they age. But they do not consider, perhaps, that because they have not given good support or even neglected their old parents, it is likely that they too, as they grow old, will have to suffer the same misfortune. Contrast this with the Buddha's teaching that children's debt to parents is so great that it can never be repaid by only material support. One should certainly give this but the support of Dhamma should also be given to them.

Are they stingy? Teach them generosity and its benefits. Perhaps their moral conduct is not good in some way? Then lead them to see the dangers of unwholesome conduct. Or maybe they lack understanding. Open the gates of Dhamma so that they understand good and evil, the causal arising of events and so on.

Only in this way can parents be repaid by their children. One's parents should be honoured—the Buddha has called them God (*Brahmā*) and it is surely better to pay homage to them with devoted service and loving-kindness, which will bring them joy in their declining years, than to worship any kind of god unknown to oneself personally. A good Buddhist thinks and acts in this way towards his parents: "I who was sustained by them, shall sustain them; I shall do their work for them; I shall keep up their family traditions; I shall make myself worthy of my inheritance; I shall make continual offerings for them when they have died." These are the Buddha's words to young Sigāla. Regarding the last, this means the well-known Buddhist practice of giving alms (to Bhikkhus and others) on death anniversaries and dedicating the merits to those who have died. In this way parents are supported even beyond this life. This is a blessing for those who are so kind and grateful, as they have the chance to make much good kamma.

Putta-dārassa saṅgaho: "cherishing one's wife and children."[10]

Surely everyone knows that this should be done. But one hears also of many cases when they are

10. In the days of the Buddha women were not as mobile socially as they are now, so he had no cause to say "cherishing one's husband and children" but this is obviously included here.

neglected or abandoned by a husband gone elsewhere. When a man has such commitments, he has the duty to support the wife and help the children. The Buddha taught young Sigāla that a husband can help his wife in five ways: by cherishing her, by not looking down on her, by not being unfaithful to her, by giving her authority in her sphere of work and by making presents to her of such things as ornaments. Any way of helpfulness which is in accord with the Dhamma is a true blessing because all such actions are good kamma—wholesome and with happy results. If done in the right spirit, "cherishing wife and children" must bring harmony into the home, and just in this life to live at peace with others is a blessing, what of the good results in lives to come?

Anākulā ca kammantā means activities and livelihood which bring no conflicts and can be attended to peacefully without mental confusion. Not only should one's work bring no conflicts but one should avoid disturbing others.

The significance of the expression will be much better appreciated by understanding that kamma (in this context meaning work) should be a means to an end (*anta*). The adjective *anākulā*—"unconflicting"—shows how the work (*kamma*) should be done to reach the end (*anta*).

Life is a state of conflict brought about by the roots of the unwholesome, greed, hatred and delusion, which are the sources of so many (*kamma*) actions. The fruits arising from this action are various kinds of sufferings and limitations, further causes for conflict. The objective in life is not to further complicate conflicts but to act, work and attend to business in a way that leads to the lessening and eventual riddance of conflicts. The emphasis is on making wholesome kamma as a means of achieving noble and desirable objectives. It is not the quality of the objective alone that decides the worth of an activity, it is the objective taken together with the means to it and related activities, which decides final worth. Thus the "means" (*kamma*) have as much importance as the "ends." To sum up this blessing: what is important here is right livelihood—that one's work leads to no harm for oneself or other beings. This kind of work everyone will agree is a blessing.

Stanza VI: *"Acts of giving, righteous living …"*

Dāna: charity, liberality, offering of gifts, etc.

The important thing here is not the act as it appears, but the intention behind it. Thus dāna may be graded as low, medium and superior according to whether the motive is selfish, unselfish or a mixture of these. The results vary accordingly both in quality and quantity.

The mental purity of the recipient and the amount of what is given, though undoubtedly important factors, are yet subsidiary to the intention motivating the offering.

Apart from the material *dāna* visibly given through the body, *dāna* may also be practised by speech and mind: a friendly smile, words of goodwill, a generous nature and a mind full of loving-kindness.

Giving also works in harmony with other good qualities and strengthens them. For instance, a generous person develops both renunciation in being able to give freely and compassion, concern to aid the plight of others. Giving is also related to moral conduct, that one gives gifts which do not conflict with the precepts. And this brings in another relationship with wisdom, for one should give wisely, not unwisely.

Finally, another division of types of giving often seen is into material offerings (such as lay people make to Bhikkhus and nuns and so make their lives possible), and the gift of Dhamma (often given by Bhikkhus and others who have learned and practised, to those who want to know). This *Dhamma-dāna* excels all other kinds of gift, since, unlike material gifts, it never wears out, instead becoming stronger with use, as well as being of benefit in future lives, besides the present one. A great blessing!

Dhammacariyā: practice of Dhamma.

"Living by the Dhamma" means making efforts to maintain and increase one's practice of the ten wholesome paths of kamma. Restraint from their evil counterparts has already been mentioned under "well-trained discipline." So here they are explained in a positive way.

1. Refraining from killing living beings implies the growth of *loving-kindness* and *compassion* in one's speech and bodily actions.
2. By not stealing (and so on) is meant the presence of *right livelihood*, a factor of the Noble Eightfold Path.
3. Right conduct in sex means that *contentment* with one's partner is strong in the mind.
4. One's speech is *truthful*.
5. It is also *harmonious* and brings people together in concord.
6. And it is *gentle* as well, so that one's words are loved by others.
7. Finally it is *meaningful*, not concerned with stupid trifles but has value for one's listeners.

8. *Renunciation* becomes stronger.
9. While *loving-kindness* is established in the emotions.
10. Finally one understands rightly and clearly about Dhamma and oneself.

In the context of the stanza the term Dhamma has the connotation of "righteousness." This is supported by a commentary which gives as a synonym, *samacariyā* (*sama*, here means "just").

Anavajjāni kammāni: blameless actions. "*Anavajjāni*": "not forbidden," "not blameworthy," "not to be shunned," "without reproach." "*Kammāni*": actions, works.

The expressions, "unconflicting types of work" and "blameless actions," are accepted as synonymous by some authors. They might be so at first glance but they differ in their emphasis.

Thus while the unconflicting types of work lay emphasis on the nature of the activities with which one is occupied, the expression "blameless actions" stresses the making of kamma which will not lead to obstacles and hindrances in the future. One could say that here the intention in the mind is stressed. The Pāli commentary bears this out when under this blessing it suggests a number of actions which are blameless, such as keeping the eight precepts on the *Uposatha* days, social services, planting gardens and groves (for public use), making bridges (again for the benefit of all).

Then there are the hospitable actions for which Buddhists are famous: the full jar of cool water to refresh thirsty travellers and the rest house giving shade which anyone may use. All such actions are praiseworthy, irrespective of one's belief—for where is kindliness not praised? It is a great blessing wherever many kindly people are found.

Stanza VII: *"Avoiding evil and abstaining ..."*

Ārati viratī pāpā: avoiding and abstaining from evil. The words *"ārati"* and *"virati"* occur together in several places in the scriptures. Taken together they mean "leaving off," "abstinence," "keeping away from," "avoiding," etc. Though the two terms have similarity of meaning they are not the same, as we shall see. Both signify effort at detachment from something unwholesome in the range of sensual pleasure, that is, the evil mentioned in the stanza. It is the difference in scope between the two terms that makes them into two distinct blessings in the Sutta. Thus the expression "avoiding and abstaining from evil," means *avoiding evil* and *abstaining from evil.*

The commentary explains avoiding evil to mean "mental non-delight" in it, a shrinking away from evil thoughts that have arisen so that they cease, having run out of fuel to burn. Only when this avoidance is not present in the mind can the fires of greed, aversion and delusion be fuelled up with the persistent flames of evil thoughts.

But abstaining from evil means "abstinence by way of bodily and verbal actions." Where mental avoidance of evil is present there will also be abstinence from it through body and speech but the presence of the latter does not guarantee the former. Why this is so is explained by the commentary when it says that abstinence may be the result of following custom or tradition. For if people do not steal, let us say, thinking "It would disgrace the family" then they have present only "abstinence as custom." A better reason for abstinence is found in the person who remembers the precepts, thinking, "Oh, I shall break that training rule." This is called "abstinence as undertaking." Best of all is "abstinence as severance" found in the Noble (*ariya*) disciple who can abstain quite naturally and without struggle because the power of evil has been weakened in his heart.

The scriptures also teach three kinds of avoiding and abstaining, namely, from wrong speech, wrong (bodily) action and wrong livelihood. This means that both of these blessings are concerned with *sīla* or morality.

Concerning this word "evil" (*pāpa*), what does it mean? Why do we say that this or that action is wrong speech, wrong (bodily) action or wrong livelihood? All the actions listed under these headings bring trouble and suffering to oneself and to others. They lead to blame from other people and for the doer of them they cause many obstacles and difficulties in the future. Here they are:

1. Wrong speech means false speech, malicious speech, harsh speech and gossip.
   Wrong bodily actions are killing living beings, taking what is not given, wrong conduct in sexual desires.
2. Wrong livelihood is one that harms others, e.g., trading in arms, slaves, intoxicants and professions involving killing, cheating, astrology or other prognosticating trickery.

Majjapānā ca saññamo: "refraining from intoxicating drinks." *Majja*: intoxicating; *pānā*: drinks. *Majja*: this is related to our English word "mad" and there is a play on intoxication and maddening which English cannot reproduce. However, everyone the world over knows the effects of alcohol and other intoxicants. Though drinks are mentioned here, anything which leads to more delusion of the mind, whether swallowed, injected or smoked should be included. A Buddhist wants a clear mind that can understand easily what is going on in his own mind and body, as well as other actions. But these besotting substances just lead to more and more foolishness. Thoroughly drunk, a person knows nothing but must suffer when he wakes. Partly drunk a person becomes capable of actions which he would be ashamed to do while sober. And carelessness from intoxication leads to the death or maiming of how many people these days? So those who are intoxicated are rightly blamed by wise men. The commentary remarks that these people are censured in this very life, get themselves an unhappy future life and when finally they return to the human state after long sub-human existences, they are born mad. This seems just enough for they madden themselves with intoxicants now, so the fruits of such kamma bring madness, a whole life without understanding. Taking all this into account an earnest follower of the Buddha should abstain completely from all intoxicants.

Appamādo ca dhammesu: "diligence in Dhamma doing"; "*a*" (a negative prefix, not) *-pamāda* (negligence and heedlessness). *Pamāda*, like *majja* in the last blessing, is also related linguistically to madness. This is the opposite of what the Buddha taught! He constantly urged people to cultivate *appamāda* or diligence. The word in Pāli has the flavour of three good qualities: effort, mindfulness and wisdom. These three go along together in anyone who tries to develop the Dhamma in himself and such a person is *appamatta*, diligent or heedful. Now here the Buddha is admonishing us to be diligent in cultivating Dhamma—all aspects of it—in ourselves.

This means we should try to protect whatever good practices we have already, and make the effort also to develop further in *dhamma*-qualities or practices. If we find any of the following in our hearts then we are slipping:

1. carelessness
2. inattentiveness
3. heedlessness
4. hanging back
5. unzealousness
6. uninterestedness
7. non-repetition (of Dhamma learned by heart)
8. non-development
9. non-cultivation
10. non-resolution
11. non-application
12. negligence

concerning the development of wholesome dhammas (*Vibhaṅga* 350). Surely diligence is a blessing!

Stanza VIII: *"Right Reverence and Humility ..."*

Gāravo: reverence. This includes the proper veneration of the Buddha, Dhamma and Sangha, and respect for parents and teachers, wise people, good persons and elders—in fact, a general high regard for everyone. Even the Buddha after his Enlightenment surveyed the world to try to find a teacher to revere. When he realized that no teacher surpassed his own attainments he then proclaimed in verse that he would live revering the Dhamma through which Enlightenment had been discovered.

And the Arahant-disciples too had reverence for the Buddha as their guide, for the Dhamma, for other senior Bhikkhus and for the way of training.

The further one has gone along the path of Dhamma the more reverence one has for it—and for others who also practice correctly. It is not that reverence grows less as one practises! This is a way of estimating one's own position, for if a lot of pride and conceit can be seen then one has not got very far!

How does one show respect or reverence? The Buddha says that one gives such a person a good seat, stands up to receive them, makes way for them and for religious teachers, one places one's hands together and bows at their feet. This is a blessing resulting in good future births and harmony in the present life.

Nivāto: humility: yet another factor which stresses the importance of having no pride. The fact that we encounter a number of "blessings" which deal with non-pride should make us realize how important humility is for the successful practice of Dhamma. The person who knows it all, who always replies "I know," who has his own theories about Dhamma, or anyone else's theories for that matter, does not have humility. Because of this he can never train under a good teacher. The Commentary gives the right attitude to have: to be lowly "like a foot-wiping cloth," "like a bull with horns cut off" or "like a snake with fangs extracted." People like this get on with Dhamma. Of course, this does not mean that one is obsequiously 'humble'—just another disguise for pride and a revolting one at that. But the wise person tries to make displays of self less and less evident. He does not advertise himself; he is not exuberant in body or speech but instead is restrained. It is interesting to note that this humility in Pāli is literally "not-wind" which ties up well with such English expressions of conceit and pride as "puffery," "vapouring," or more colloquially "hot air" and "gas."

Santuṭṭhī: contentment. This implies acceptance of Conditions and situations as they arise, with equanimity and without grumbling.

This is a quality which Bhikkhus must have, as the commentary emphasizes when it does not mention lay people at all here. This is a much needed quality in those parts of the world and among those families where there is affluence. Contentment spells peace of mind for the person who has it; craving more and more spells out the opposite. What should one be content with? With enough clothes, enough food, enough living room and enough medicines. But then what is enough and what is excess? "Enough" gives one little trouble to keep and maintain but more than that brings anxiety and worry. This blessing should also not be misunderstood as counsel not to make an effort in life. Bhikkhus do not have to possess many things for happiness in their life but lay people need much more. Lay people must make effort to obtain what is necessary for a happy life without poverty and starvation. Everyone has to decide for oneself whether possessions will bring more happiness or more trouble. Being able to know this clearly is an aspect of wisdom.

Kataññutā: gratitude. Literally, this is "knowing what has been done," that is, remembering what others have done for oneself. The Buddha has said: "Two sorts of people are hard to find in the world: one who first does (something kind or helpful), and one who is grateful and recognizes (that kindness)." Without this quality a person forgets parents, relatives, friends, teachers and those who teach him Dhamma; he turns his back on them just when they could be helped by him or when they are in need of aid. A selfish person seems to try to isolate himself from the world's web. "I alone am important," he says, and forgets all the benefit derived from others. On the other hand the grateful person makes for harmony and peace. How many good things have we obtained through others in this life and how many are we grateful for and then express our gratitude in speech and action?

Kālena dhammasavanaṃ: "timely hearing of Dhamma," means that the occasion for hearing the teachings of the Buddha should be well-timed. Hearing of Dhamma should be opportune.

Obviously, the hearing of Dhamma will be more profitable if regularly attended to at times when one has healthy body and mind: when one is exhausted, except perhaps during disease or suffering, this may lead to sleepiness, and so it is not suitable.

Some of the excellent general occasions for the hearing of the teachings are:

1. Sacred days such as the Full Moon days, or during Buddhist festivals.
2. When disease and suffering make one thoughtful enough to want to understand the truth of suffering (*dukkha*), and ready enough to find a way out of the sufferings.
3. When the mind is specially inclined towards the teachings, as when one does concentrated meditation practice for some time.
4. When evil thoughts have invaded the mind but have not yet fully taken possession of it.
5. A special meaning of "*savana*" (hearing) these days is to know Dhamma from book-study. In the

Buddha's time knowledge was gained only by hearing but now it is more by way of books. This should also find a place here.

6. At the time of death, when concentration of mind can condition a happy rebirth or may even help attain one of the Paths and Fruits.

Regarding the suitable time of the day, no definite rules can be laid down, for what suits one may not suit another. It is proper to take into consideration the following general points:

1. There should not be any undue tiredness of body or mind, for this distracts attention and makes one sleepy.
2. There should be sufficient freedom from personal business or domestic worries.
3. The mind should be in a receptive state.
4. The mind also should be free from the influences of all kinds of drugs and intoxicants.

Timely hearing of the Dhamma is a great blessing since because of it the five hindrances can be abandoned even while one sits there, and the ten fetters too, so that even the three kinds of taints may be exhausted and Arahantship won through listening attentively. Even if such attainments do not occur, then one comes to know Dhamma which one had not heard before, while what one had heard is learned in detail. With such a store of Dhamma one can apply it to one's life for one's own benefit and the happiness of others. A great blessing!

Stanza IX: *"Patience, Meekness when Corrected ..."*

Khantī: This is an important virtue, in fact one of the highest. It can be translated as patience but it includes the virtues of forbearance, forgiveness and tolerance. It finds expression as a serene attitude towards stresses in oneself and outside, which enables a person to accept with equanimity the flow of events. Because of this the impressions entering the mind from the sense doors cannot upset the peace reigning there; so one goes on serenely with the work in hand. Though all sorts of upsetting situations occur and send their disturbing messages to the mind, it does not become heated. In fact with even a little of this virtue the mind becomes cool, clean and calm, like a refreshing pool of crystal clear water, quite unlike the minds of most people, which can rightly be compared to a pot of boiling soup or a cup of water with swirls of colour in it.

A person who practises patience has a "cool heart," the mark of a person who has applied the Dhamma to his life. "Cool-heartedness," not worried, flustered or impatient, marks the good Buddhist, while "hot-heartedness" shows how little of Dhamma a person has in his heart.

Khantī is one of the *pāramitās* (perfections) which one who aspires to Enlightenment must perfect to a far greater degree than just not being impatient or impetuous. This we know from that famous story of the *Bodhisatta's* life when he was the Preacher of Patience, a monk living harmlessly in the forest who was slaughtered by a maddened king, about which it is said in that story:

In olden times there was a monk,
Of patience he was paragon;
He kept his patience even when
The king of Kāsi murdered him.

Even if our patience is not tried by such extreme events, still we have to encounter heat and cold, hunger and thirst, various insects and so on which attack this body, and the sharp words of others which seem to attack the ego; then there are occasions for being patient about time, and how many times for being patient with the frailties of other people? But the basis of all patience is to be patient with oneself.

Patience is thus the foundation of *mettā* (loving-kindness). It is reckoned as a great power; and the strength of those who have patience is often praised in Buddhist writings.

Sovacassatā: the meaning given in the Commentaries is "one who can easily be addressed, spoken to or advised" and it further means "a person who can be corrected." Also implied are the qualities of tolerance of criticism directed at oneself and courtesy and gratitude in accepting advice.

The Commentary says that a person who is meek when corrected has the chance to learn Dhamma, which is the opposite of the person who is "difficult to speak to." The latter "indulge in prevarication, silence or think up virtues and vices." Prevarication is only a fancy word for lying, the method used by some people when they are admonished. Another way is sullen silence, while the third is blaming the adviser by charging him with faults or else praising one's own virtue. People like this are difficult to train; others find them hard to get on with. One should examine oneself to find out whether or not one has the blessing of being meek when corrected.

Obviously a gentle person will only need to be told to do a thing gently: he is like a well-bred horse, needing just a soft touch, unlike an obstinate beast, which only responds to harsh treatment. He is a thoroughbred with the attributes of broadmindedness of outlook, instant acceptance of good advice and habitual courtesy in manners and speech.

Samaṇānañ ca dassanaṃ: "seeing monks or holy men." *Samaṇa* (lit., one who has made oneself peaceful), a monk, a holy man. The Buddha was often addressed as Samaṇa, by those who were not his followers.

In the ordinary sense *dassanaṃ* means "seeing" with the physical eye. But generally the expression signifies more than mere "seeing," even when used in the restricted sense of seeing in the ordinary way. The underlying sense is conveyed when the act of visual "seeing" has as its objectives holy persons of purity and real worth. "Seeing" is generally performed with the desire to pay respects to them. This is also the sense of the modern Hindi word *darshan*. For a Buddhist, however, it is not enough just to gaze with devotion and perform acts of worship. So the expression means much more than mere "meeting" or "seeing." It involves mind, speech and body in a harmonious synthesis:

1. A desire to meet holy persons, particularly the monks and nuns following the teachings of the Buddha.
2. Making genuine efforts to visit them at their monasteries or making use of any opportunity available to pay one's respects to them such as when they are on their rounds for almsfood or during their visits to friends and relatives, or when one is able to receive them reverently at one's house.

3. Deriving inspiration from their company.

There is no better company than holy persons, whose very presence spreads a purifying aura and inspires a constructive approach to one's problems. Such company is an antidote to evil ways of life besides leading one to discover for oneself spiritual treasures in due course.

In the deeper sense *dassana* means "seeing" with the mental eye, e.g., *ñāṇadassana* (insight through knowledge) and *dhamma-dassana* (rightly understanding the Doctrine). So in the deepest sense *dassana* means perception of the Noble Truths. All those deeper meanings can come about through simply "seeing the monks."

Kālena dhammasākacchā: "timely discussion on the Dhamma."

As Dhamma is a profound subject it needs sincere effort to understand it properly and grasp it for practical use in life. This can be made easier through discussions with others who have a thorough knowledge of the theory and practice of Dhamma.

Discussions should be well-timed. The right times for discussions with intelligent, wise and experienced people should not be missed, even though it means personal inconvenience. Still, one should remember that discussions would not be opportune if the convenience of the other person is neglected.

It is particularly timely to discuss the Dhamma when one's mind is troubled either by defilements of the mind such as uncertainty, or by exterior troubles in the family, at work or in any kind of relationship.

Stanza X: *"Self-Restraint and Holy Life ..."*

Tapo literally means "heat." Its brahmanical meaning was "ascetic practices," which the Buddha showed were useless for the attainment of deliverance. Though he denounced the torment of one's own body, the Buddha used this word to mean self-control, as with the restraint of one's sense faculties. When these are restrained then such unwholesome mental states as covetousness and grief have no chance to appear. But "tapo" was used in another sense by the Buddha to mean vigorous efforts, the sort which a Bhikkhu has to make if he is to win Enlightenment. It is the kind of effort which *burns up* the defilements.

Brahmacariyaṃ: holy life. The general Buddhist meaning is "the best life," but in some places it means "the Buddha's Dispensation" (*sāsana*) while elsewhere it is "the monk's ideal life" (*samaṇa-dhamma*). Here it can include these two besides the more common meaning of "leading a holy life" which implies abstaining from sex. With *brahmacariyā* may also be included the practice of the Four Sublime States (*brahma-vihāra*), viz. *mettā* (loving-kindness), *karuṇā* (compassion), *muditā* (altruistic joy) and *upekkhā* (equanimity).

The word *brahmacariyā*, while including all aspects of Dhamma-practice in its scope, emphasizes moral purity. Through the study and practice of Dhamma one attains self-control; and an important part of this is sex control, which energy empowers the clear meditative mind as well as providing the drive for beneficial social activities.

Sensual desire generally is a cause of many lives and much suffering. As sexual desire is a concentrated form of sensuality, and so is the cause of much trouble, the Buddha has shown how it can be checked first by precepts (*sīla*), and then through meditation. For the lay followers, sex is limited to that allowed in the third of the five precepts, while for Bhikkhus complete sexual abstinence is necessary. Bhikkhus are bound to practise it strictly and even lay followers may undertake the precept of sexual abstinence if they wish. Worldly life, though not much help for this practice, does not make it impossible. Buddhists observe this vow on the Uposatha days, and some who are endowed with strong self-control and a firm determination to advance in meditation, practise it all the time while engaged in the general round of worldly duties.

Ariyasaccāna-dassanaṃ, "seeing the Noble Truths," i.e., the Four Noble Truths, which constitute the central pillar of the Buddha's Dhamma and of which all other Buddhist doctrines are a preparation or elaboration. The Four Noble Truths are the briefest factual description of experience during life. They constitute the unique and vital discovery made by the Buddha which was announced by him in his very first discourse.

The truths are:

I. That all forms of existence are subject to suffering (this is the Truth of Suffering: *dukkha-sacca*).[11]

II. That craving (*taṇhā*) is the cause of suffering (this is the Truth of the Cause of Suffering: *dukkha-samudaya-sacca*).

---

11. One should remember that the English word "suffering" does not include all *dukkha*. All experience is impermanent, unreliable or insecure and therefore *dukkha*. Pleasant experience too is *dukkha* but it cannot be called suffering.

III. That the removal of the cause results in the absence of the effect (this is the Truth of the Cessation of Suffering: *dukkha-nirodha-sacca*).

IV. That the path is the means to attain the cessation of suffering (this is the Truth of the Path, the Noble Eightfold Path, for the cessation of suffering: *magga-sacca*).

The eight steps of the Noble Eightfold Path are:

1. *sammā-diṭṭhi*: right view
2. *sammā-saṅkappa*: right intention
3. *sammā-ājīva:* right livelihood
4. *sammā-kammanta*: right action
5. *sammā-ājīva:* right livelihood
6. *sammā-vāyāma:* right (mental) effort
7. *sammā-sati:* right mindfulness
8. *sammā-samādhi:* right concentration.[12]

These eight steps are usually grouped into the following three divisions:

A. *Sīla* (morality): 3, 4, and 5.
B. *Samādhi* (mental concentration): 6, 7 and 8.
C. *Paññā* (deep wisdom): 1 and 2.

Knowledge of these truths may be intellectual or by way of realization. The former variety of knowledge, as it is intellectual or hearsay evidence, only helps understanding the formulation of these truths, which still remain to be realized. The knowledge gained in this way remains limited as relative truth.

---

12. For a systematic description of the path see Ledi Sayādaw, *The Noble Eightfold Path and Its Factors Explained*, BPS Wheel Publication No. 245/247.

The knowledge based on direct perception is that of realization: it is the "knowledge penetrated by truth" (*paṭivedha-ñāṇa*). The former type of knowledge is termed "mundane" (*lokiya*) and the latter "supramundane" (*lokuttara*).

As "mundane knowledge," the Four Noble Truths are generally perceived as separate events; nevertheless their understanding helps to dispel certain prejudices and wrong beliefs. In the supramundane stage all four truths are simultaneously realized: whoever realizes suffering, also realizes its origin, its cessation and the path to its cessation. Though at first one has an intellectual appreciation of them—for certainly this is also a blessing—here direct perception is meant, the former usually leading to the latter.

The expression means the perception of the Four Noble Truths at work in life. This insight results in the realization of the facts of (1) suffering (*dukkha*), (2) its roots in the cravings of *lobha, dosa* and *moha* (greed, hatred and delusion), (3) its extinction through the exhaustion of the cravings and (4) the technique of the conquest. Once direct insight arises, one arrives at the doorway to the Final Goal.

Nibbāna-sacchikiriyā: "the realization of Nibbāna." Nibbāna, the Final Goal, is a blessed state of freedom from desire, of freedom from greed, hatred and delusion, of perfect safety from the vicissitudes of existence, of bliss that is resplendent, of knowledge that is supreme, in brief, a state that is perfection itself.

In life, one is plagued by desires; in Nibbāna, all desires are extinguished and all clinging is nullified. In life, one lives in a forest of conflicting views and theories: in Nibbāna all these vanish under the direct perception of truth, just as the dew vanishes with the direct touch of the sun's rays.

The state of Nibbāna, which is supramundane (*lokuttara*), is beyond the power of language to describe, for words can only convey *relatively* true concepts. Therefore, it is beyond the power of anyone, even the Supreme Buddha, to describe or define Nibbāna except by using negation and occasionally more positive imagery. Hence, the Buddha has not described Nibbāna at any length although he uses similes sometimes for effect.

The attainment of Nibbāna is the most excellent achievement, needing a strong determination backed by strenuous endeavours in the right way. These endeavours must be patiently and perseveringly directed towards the eradication of the roots of evil bound up with life, namely, *lobha* (greed), *dosa* (hatred) and *moha* (delusion). These evils, rooted in ignorance (*avijjā*), generate strong fetters (*saṃyojana*) which tie beings to the painful circle of suffering, the wheel of existence, the round of birth, death and rebirth. The fetters are ten in number:

1. *sakkāyadiṭṭhi:* belief in the permanence of personality;
2. *vicikicchā:* irrational doubts;
3. *sīlabbataparāmāsa:* clinging to rituals and superstitions;
4. *kāma-rāga:* craving for sensual enjoyment;
5. *vyāpāda:* ill-will;
6. *rūpa-rāga:* craving for existence in fine-material worlds;
7. *arūpa-rāga*: craving for existence in worlds without material form;
8. *māna:* conceit;
9. *uddhacca:* restlessness;
10. *avijjā:* ignorance.

Those possessed of all the ten fetters are termed ordinary people (*puthujjana*). We are those ordinary people who are in the stormy ocean of existence (*saṃsāra*), feverishly twitching to the tune of sensual cravings while tightly bound to the wheel of suffering. We are prisoners in chains, chains riveted by our cravings.

The dissolution of these "fetters" is the highest aim of the Buddha's teaching. Though the effort needed for this is very great, the resulting fruit is sweet beyond compare. Once the right course is found, further progress is assured. The right method is mental culture through reflection, meditation and concentration. The resulting insight (*vipassanā*) is the solvent of all fetters, dissolving them away.

The dissolution of the "first three fetters" makes one a *sotāpanna* (stream-winner). This means success in shifting from the stormy ocean of life (*saṃsāra*) to the cool and steady "stream" that unmistakably leads to Nibbāna, the release. This is the first stage of Nobility. With the attainment of it, one is known as an Ariya, a Noble One. In the next stage, the next two fetters are weakened and the Noble One becomes a *sakadāgāmī* (once-returner to this world). The destruction of the next two fetters makes the Noble One an *anāgāmi* (non-returner). Freedom from all ten fetters makes one an Arahant, a Perfect One, a Fully Liberated One. He has attained the highest, that is, Nibbāna, and after death there is no more rebirth for him.

The Buddha is an Arahant as he has destroyed all the fetters. He is more than that too, for he reached the goal by a longer and more strenuous path with the object of amply profiting the world through his supreme wisdom and compassion.

The Buddha and the Arahants, unlike ordinary people, make no more mental-formations or kamma. They stand with rock-like firmness, unshaken by the winds and storms all around. They are beyond the clutches of any temptations: they are delivered of all evils, are perfectly pure and holy and full of supreme understanding. They have achieved the Goal, Nibbāna. They live only for the period necessary to expend their kammic momentum left from the past. At the end of that, as no more kamma fruits (*kamma-vipāka*) remain, they attain *Parinibbāna*, no more to return to rebirth anywhere.

There are obviously two aspects of Nibbāna:

1. *Sa-upādi-sesa-nibbāna*, Nibbāna with the groups of personality still remaining, such as the Buddha when he taught for 45 years, or an Arahant living.
2. *An-upādi-sesa-nibbāna*, Nibbāna with no more psycho-physical elements existing, i.e., the Parinibbāna of the Buddha or an Arahant.

One often hears a strange question: Who or what attains Nibbāna after the final death? The question is meaningless as there are neither any kamma-resultants nor any of the five groups (*pañcakkhandhā*) of the psycho-physical being left; so the question does not arise as to who or what "enters" Nibbāna. To explain this more fully one should know about one's "self" and what this means.

The Buddha's analysis of personality reveals five groups (*khandha*) as making up a human being: *rūpakkhandha* (physical body), *vedanākkhandha* (feelings), *saññākkhandha* (perceptions), *saṅkhārakkhandha* (mental formations and their fruits) and *viññāṇakkhandha* (consciousness). A common classification is the grouping of these five into two sections: *nāma* (mind, i.e., the psychological part of personality) comprising the last four, and *rūpa* (body, i.e., the physical aspect of personality), the first group. All these are characterized by the three qualities common to all living beings (impermanence, suffering and not-self). And as there is nothing in the human person outside these five, a human being is in reality without a permanent ego-entity, self or soul. He is like a bubble of water, or a cart on the road, things which give the impression of being entities because of the combination of certain factors, but which have no permanent substance to endure forever.

There are two aspects of truth (*sacca*), namely,

1. the conventional truth (*vohāra-sacca* or *sammuti-sacca*) and
2. the ultimate truth (*paramattha-sacca*).
   The former means "things as they appear" and the latter, "things as they really are."

The Buddha, in his discourses, while addressing ordinary people or while expounding the common-sense viewpoint, generally spoke of conventional truth. Thus in this Sutta the term *attā*, self, (see stanza III), is used only as a conventional mode of speech, meaning "the human being as he appears." In the ultimate sense the personality is a flux, ever-changing and never the same even for two consecutive fractions of a moment. This is the doctrine of *anattā*. It is a unique Buddhist discovery—in fact the most revolutionary discovery ever made in the field of human personality. Without a proper grasp of its import, Buddhism will be understood only superficially.

The conventional recognition of a self as a convenient mode of speech, however, should not lead people astray into belief in the existence of a "higher self." There is no "higher self" or soul in the ultimate sense, for no "self" of any kind, higher or lower, here or hereafter, can be found. That is why the Buddha laid emphasis on "selflessness" (*anattā*) and classed it as one of the three fundamental characteristics of all living beings, including human personality.

The proper study for a man is himself, for once the emptiness of self is understood, all the rest becomes easy to grasp. As tersely explained in the *Visuddhimagga*, according to ultimate truth:

There is suffering but no sufferer,
There are deeds, but no doer,
There is Nibbāna but none to enter it,
There is the Path, but no traveller on it.

Yet with this direct view of truth, in which personality finds no foothold at all, the Buddha did not ignore the truth of the conventional self. He gave it the recognition it merited, and used it as a base for directing the individual ultimately to the realization of the truth of "non-personality" (*anattā*). This is where the expression *attasammāpaṇidhi* "one's self rightly directed" (stanza III) eventually leads. Thus, evil tendencies and practices (really existing because of the love for or lust about "self") give way to the wholesome tendencies and practices, once the delusion of self is penetrated.

From the very start, one should know that the "self" is accepted merely as a convenient or conventional designation and that its apparent reality can certainly be understood as a delusion, once its non-existence in the ultimate sense is realized. The very fact of starting the life's journey in this way becomes the "act of directing or setting oneself in the right course by oneself." Though there may be external help available, the emphasis is on the "right direction" and self-reliance. All available wholesome assistance should be used but not too much dependence should be shown to any aid apart from that springing from within one's self. So Nibbāna is not attained by any person (= self) in the highest sense.

Nibbāna-sacchikiriyā: the expression means the very realization of Nibbāna or at least an actual glimpse of it, which can be had by no less a person than a *sotāpanna* (the winner of the stream leading to Nibbāna).

It may here be pointed out that the expression "the realization of Nibbāna" implies that by one's own efforts one reaches the goal. Through determination and perseverance in the right direction the goal is reached, and not through grace: it is not a "Gift from the Heavens," but the fruit of one's supreme endeavours. In brief, the goal is one's own earnings: verily Nibbāna is well earned. Blessed is the person who earns it.

Stanza XI: *"Though Touched by Worldly Circumstances ..."*

Phuṭṭhassa lokadhammehi, cittaṃ yassa na kampati: "a mind which does not waver when touched by worldly conditions." Worldly conditions, inseparable from life, are eight in number: *lābha* (gain), *alābhā* (loss), *ayasa* (disgrace), *yasa* (fame), *nindā* (blame), *pasaṃsā* (praise), *sukha* (happiness, pleasure) and *dukkha* (pain). While ordinary people grasp the pleasant halves of these pairs and reject the unpleasant (which means they use greed and hatred), Noble Ones, especially Arahants, are not shaken by either of the halves. We, as ordinary people, should try to develop more equanimity towards gains and loss, and so on.

Asokaṃ (sorrowless), *virajaṃ* (unstained by passion) and *khemaṃ* (secure from sensuality) are the attributes of an Arahant. These describe the mental state of a Fully Liberated One. The mind of such a person is unique—free from disturbances, purified of passion and finished with sensuality, it is calm and serene, without the storms of desires and the waves of worries. The worldly conditions (*lokadhamma*) do not sway him; he stands firmly, witnessing but untouched by the changeful and sorrowful drama of life going on all around.

Stanza XII: *"Since by Acting in This Way ..."*

This stanza concludes the Sutta.

The fulfilment of these blessings is shown by

invincibility everywhere
perfect happiness and security.

This is the most sublime of all attainments, the Everest of human achievements, Nibbāna in this life.

Chapter IV

The Highroad of Blessings

I. *The Thirty-eight Blessings*

Stanza I

The Buddha was asked:
    What are the highest Blessings in life?
The Blessed One replied:
    The Supreme Blessings are:

Stanza II

1. *Asevanā ca bālānaṃ*: Not associating with fools.
2. *Paṇḍitānañ ca sevanā*: Associating with the wise.
3. *Pūjā ca pūjanīyānaṃ*: Reverencing those worthy of respect.

Stanza III

4. *Paṭirūpadesavāso*: Residence in a suitable locality.
5. *Pubbe ca kata-puññatā*: Having made merit in the past.
6. *Attasammāpaṇidhi:* One's mind properly directed.

Stanza IV

7. *Bahusaccañ*: Profound learning.
8. *Bahusippañ*: Proficiency in one's work.
9. *Vinayo ca susikkhito*: Well-trained moral discipline.
10. *Subhāsitā ca yā vācā*: Gracious kindly speech.

Stanza V

11. *Mātā-pitu upaṭṭhānaṃ*: Giving support to parents.
12. *Putta-dārassa saṅgaho*: Cherishing wife and children.
13. *Anākulā ca kammantā*: Business pursuits, peaceful and free from conflicts.

Stanza VI

14. *Dānañ*: Acts of giving.
15. *Dhammacariyā*: Conduct according to Dhamma.
16. *Ñātakānañ ca saṅgaho*: Helping one's relatives.
17. *Anavajjāni kammāni*: Blameless actions.

Stanza VII

18. *Ārati pāpā*: Shunning evil.
19. *Virati pāpā*: Abstaining from evil.
20. *Majjapānā ca saññamo*: Refraining from intoxicants.
21. *Appamādo ca dhammesu*: Diligence in practice of what is Dhamma.

Stanza VIII

22. *Gāravo*: Reverence.
23. *Nivāto*: Humility.
24. *Santuṭṭhi*: Contentment.
25. *Kataññutā*: Gratefulness.
26. *Kālena dhammasavanaṃ*: Timely hearing of the Dhamma.

Stanza IX

27. *Khantī*: Patience.
28. *Sovacassatā*: Meekness (amenability) when corrected.
29. *Samaṇānañ ca dassanaṃ*: Meeting (seeing) monks.

30. *Kālena dhammasākacchā*: Discussing the Dhamma at the proper time.

Stanza X

31. *Tapo*: Energetic self-restraint.
32. *Brahmacariyaṃ:* Holy and chaste life.
33. *Ariyasaccāna-dassanaṃ*: Insight into the Noble Truths.
34. *Nibbāna sacchikiriyā*: Realization of Nibbāna.

Stanza XI

35. *Phuṭṭhassa lokadhammehi cittaṃ yassa na kampati:* A mind unshaken by the ups and downs of life.
36. *Asokaṃ*: Freedom from sorrow.
37. *Virajaṃ*: Freedom from defilements of passion.
38. *Khemaṃ*: Perfect security.

Stanza XII

Etādisāni katvāna, sabbattham-aparājitā sabbattha sotthiṃ gacchanti:

Those who have acted in this way cannot be defeated and always live in safety.

II. General Review

The thirty-eight blessings detailed in the Mahā Maṅgala Sutta are not arranged in random order. Their arrangement is strictly logical and their sequence is natural and progressive.

Up to this point we have dealt with the various issues individually because an analytic study was necessary for the proper understanding of the subject.

Now, with the perspective of the entire Sutta, we are in a position to consider the subject as a whole. This enlarged view, while giving us a chance to appreciate the cultural integrity of the Sutta, also gives an understanding of the synthesis of its thirty-eight constituents. These constituents are so arranged that they not only follow one another in proper sequence, but they also group themselves into categories which are themselves in the progressive order of development in Dhamma.

Before we pass on to a systematic classification of these blessings, it will be refreshing to read the following comments on the Sutta, adapted from Shway Yoe,[13] who is quoting the Christian Bishop Bigandet:

"Within a narrow compass, the Buddha has condensed an abridgment of almost all moral virtues. The first portion of these precepts contains injunctions to shun all that may prove an impediment to the practice of good works. The second part inculcates the necessity of regulating one's mind and intention for a regular discharge of the duties incumbent on each man in his separate station. Then follows a recommendation to bestow assistance on parents, relatives and all men in general. Next to that we find recommended the virtues of humility, resignation,[14] gratitude and patience. After this, the Teacher insists on the necessity of studying the Law, visiting the religious, conversing on religious subjects. When this is done, one is recommended to study with great attention the four great Truths, and keep the mind's eye ever fixed on the happy state of

---

13. Shway Yoe, *The Burman: His Life and Notions*. London: Macmillan & Co., 1896, p. 571.

14. But "resignation" is not in the Sutta, nor a virtue recommended by the Buddha. See Stanzas VIII–IX.

Nibbāna, which, though as yet distant, ought never to be lost sight of. Thus prepared, one must be bent upon acquiring the qualifications befitting the true sage who would remain firm, fearless and unmoved, even in the midst of the ruins of the crumbling universe; the Buddhist sage ever remains calm, composed and unshaken among all the vicissitudes of life. There is again clearly pointed out the final end to be arrived at, viz. that of perfect mental stability. This state is the foreshadowing of 'Nibbāna.'"

III. A Synthetic View

The ingredients of the Mahā Maṅgala Sutta, because of their moral excellence and practical appeal, are capable of many classifications. Thus, the thirty-eight blessings can be presented in a variety of combinations. The author, after thinking deeply over the possible groupings, has arrived at a pattern worked out by himself. This classification is based on practical considerations and is expected to be generally useful.

Before we present our own classification, it is proposed to offer another, the essential feature of which is the division of the Sutta into the three classical sections, namely, *sīla* (moral culture), *samādhi* (mental culture) and *paññā* (wisdom). The credit for developing this admirable classification goes to Maṅgala U Ba Than, the very honorific prefix to whose name is significant of the excellent work done by him in Burma in popularizing the teaching and the practice of the *Maṅgala* Sutta. He groups the first twenty-one maṅgalas under *sīla* and divides them into five groups. These ensure the basic training of the individual as well as assisting with the discharge of his obligations in the social sphere. The next nine *maṅgalas* are classed under *samādhi* as aspects of mental culture. The last eight maṅgalas come under *paññā* and are either the practice towards or the fruit of wisdom and insight.

Steady and regular practice of the twenty-one *maṅgalas* grouped under *sīla* brings the utmost happiness, prosperity and satisfaction possible in the human state. These admirable achievements are not only adequately stabilized and ensured against possible setbacks, but are also further enhanced by the practice of the nine *maṅgalas* grouped under *samādhi*. The last eight *maṅgalas* grouped under *paññā* assist the progressive realization of the highest wisdom.

The above classification is schematically represented below:

I. *Sīla*: moral culture (21 *maṅgalas*)	1. Fundamental rules: *maṅgalas* 1–6
A. The preparation	2. Essential training of the senses, body, mind & speech: *maṅgalas* 7–10
B. Compulsory obligations	3. foundation of domestic order: *maṅgalas* 11–13
	4. Social welfare: *maṅgalas* 14–17
C. Vigilance	5. Protection against evil: *maṅgalas* 18–21
II. *Samādhi*: mental culture	*maṅgalas* 22–27
(9 *maṅgalas*)	*maṅgalas* 28–30
III. *Paññā*: wisdom culture	*maṅgalas* 31–36
(8 *maṅgalas*)	*maṅgalas* 37–38

IV. Our Classification

The Mahā Maṅgala Sutta, a well-charted course of personal culture and progress, is an excellent guide for reaching even the highest goal. It is a four-sectioned ladder which helps one to climb step by step to the zenith of noble achievements.

The ideal of life is deliverance from fears and insecurities. This is achieved through steady, strenuous effort, and righteous wayfaring in the world. Such a great venture as this obviously needs adequate preparation and thorough training. The Mahā Maṅgala Sutta indicates not only the course of the preparatory training but also safely guides the individual through the journey of life and ultimately leads him to the secure haven of Nibbāna.

The first five *maṅgalas* (1–5) provide material for the foundation of life's building. The sixth (6) gives the necessary plan for the construction work, while the next four (7–10) complete the structure. In this way the building is made ready to house the other *maṅgalas*. This constitutes the phase of preparation.

The next phase is concerned with how the building already prepared is occupied. The first seven *maṅgalas* (11–17) of this deal with the proper discharge of domestic duties and social obligations. The next three (18–20) are a matter of personal conduct, and the one (21) following these aims at conserving the progress hitherto achieved through the practice of all the twenty *maṅgalas* mentioned so far. The next five *maṅgalas* (22–26) are the cultivation of the higher virtues which are absolutely essential for venturing into the cultivation of the Dhamma's highest aspects. Thus through the operation of the last sixteen *maṅgalas* the residence of life, prepared by the first ten becomes a workshop producing the goods of worldly obligations and the cultivation of benevolent feelings. This is the phase of "wayfaring in the world which transforms the building into a temple of life."

The next stage is spiritual growth. This invites the occupation of the temple by the most refined and exalted *maṅgalas.* The cultivation of two *maṅgalas* (27–28) leads to ability in the practice of the spiritual life and the next two (29–30) make contact with those leading a religious life. Then four more *maṅgalas* (31–34) open the gates of realization of the Dhamma. And the last four *maṅgalas* (35–38) constitute the Great Awakening, which transforms the temple into a lighthouse for humanity. This is the ultimate benefit of Dhamma-practice, the signs of which are the invincibility of such a person and Supreme Bliss.

Schematically listed the above phases are:

I. The Preparation:
1. Laying the Right Foundation through
    a. Suitable associations: *maṅgalas* 1–3
    b. A good place to live: *maṅgalas* 4
    c. Past merits: *maṅgalas* 5
2. Right Planning: *maṅgalas* 6
3. Right Training: *maṅgalas* 7–10

II. Wayfaring in the World:
1. Basic Responsibilities: *maṅgalas* 10–13
2. Social Obligations: *maṅgalas* 14–17
3. Self-Protection: *maṅgalas* 18–20
4. Conservation of Personal Progress: *maṅgalas* 21
5. Cultivation of Higher Qualities: *maṅgalas* 22–26

III. Spiritual Growth:
1. Spiritual Eligibility: *maṅgalas* 26–27
2. Contact with Religious Life: *maṅgalas* 29–30
3. On the Path: *maṅgalas* 31–34

4. The Fruit: *maṅgalas* 35–38

IV. The Conclusion of Life: The Summum Bonum:

1. Perfect invincibility of the person
2. Durable happiness.

A comparison of the above classification with that of Maṅgala U Ba Than shows several points of contact. The major agreement is in the phase of preparation, which in both cases is taken up by the first ten *maṅgalas.* Also the terminal sections in both cases are identical.

An examination of our classification makes it evident that section one of the Sutta is concerned with preparation for the second section, which in turn is a preparation for section number three. The fourth section is the final result.

Each of these sections has several stages. The last stage of the first section qualifies the person to enter the second section of the worldly journey, and the last stage of the second section brings the pilgrim right to the threshold of the third section. The final stage of the third section spells the supreme realization of the highest aim that people can aspire to. The fourth phase is the goal itself.

The traveller through the above sections is really a pilgrim who takes up the journey of life with a definite plan covering bodily, verbal and mental activities. His object is to make of life a happy and moral means to a glorious end. The Mahā Maṅgala Sutta provides the map which takes the pilgrim safely through life's journey to the final destination so that he gains deliverance from *dukkha* and the delusions of existence.

The eleven stanzas, comprising the reply to the issue raised in the first stanza, are apportioned to the four sections as follows:

1. The Preparation: First three stanzas.
2. Wayfaring in the World: Next four stanzas.
3. The Religious Life: Next three stanzas.
4. The Highest Goal: Last stanza.

The position of Wayfaring in the World between the stages of Preparation and that of the Religious Life, while it does not mean that marriage is essential for all people at some period in life, does lay emphasis on the cultivation of moral principles and in the discharge of social and familial obligations. According to the Buddha and in contrast with the four stages of Hindu life, marriage is not a compulsory institution, though it provides sometimes a fruitful field for the cultivation of certain virtues and so appears here as an intermediate phase which can be utilized as a training ground for entrance upon the third phase of spiritual values. Thus marriage is an optional part of the second section of life. As a means to a desirable end it is commendable, but if accepted as an end in itself, it clogs the wheels of progress and becomes a sort of a labyrinth beset with passions and crowded with peculiar obstacles, which do not easily allow the pilgrim a chance to find the path leading to awakening. Therefore, those who can practice the necessary *maṅgalas* of this stage without entering into matrimonial bondage, as monks and nuns, for instance, are free to do so, the emphasis being on the cultivation of the associated virtues and the adequate discharge of certain obligations expected of the pilgrim. However, in case marriage is excluded from the program, the question of obligations due to wife and children obviously does not arise, as the pilgrim is quite free from this burden.

CHAPTER V

CONCLUSION

Usually human beings are heavily burdened, fettered with the weighty chains riveted by themselves, the chains of fears and superstitions, dogmas and rituals. Egoistic tendencies worked by the forces of greed, hatred and delusion bring about this bondage. Bound by these self-created chains, human beings suffer repeated difficulties, hardships and miseries, which rob people of self-confidence and courage. The result is belief in prayers and priests, rites and rituals, sacrifices and sacraments, speculations and the supernatural, all prompting slavish dependence on extraneous agencies and forces, imaginary or real. Thus the mind of man is entombed by the prison walls of his own making.

The Buddha was moved by great compassion at the sight of the pitiable condition of humanity drowning in its own blind beliefs. He sounded the clarion call of freedom and showed the right way of breaking through the self-made crust of superstitions smothering individual initiative, confidence and courage. His Mahā Maṅgala Sutta is a masterly antidote to all blind beliefs and superstitions.

When approached to declare the "*maṅgalāni*" or "auspicious signs," he enumerated instead the "acts of blessedness," thus bringing about a psychological revolution in the beliefs of many people.

Every section of the Sutta is a storehouse full of practical wisdom. Precious ideas and valuable counsel are packed in every line in condensed form so that their expansion is really necessary. Just as letters were micro-photographed during the war to reduce freight in air shipment and then "blown up" before delivery, so the thoughts and ideas behind the factors of the Mahā Maṅgala Sutta have to be expanded for easy study and understanding.

It should, however, be pointed out that, though the essentials of the enlarged picture will not change at different times and places, yet certain factors, such as the colour of the picture and the texture of the materials used, may differ. That is why the practical exposition of the Sutta is sure to vary under different circumstances, without altering the central values.

In the eleven stanzas of the Sutta is given counsel which can make anyone an ideal citizen. There are instructions which prepare people excellently well for a fruitful journey through life. Further counsel progressively matures the individual till he successfully passes from the worldly state to the sphere of higher virtues and certain spiritual experiences. These in due course lead to perfect liberation. Thus the phases of preparation, worldly life, religious life and spiritual consummation follow one another in logical sequence. In this way all the due obligations are adequately discharged. The ultimate fruits are flawless happiness and perfect security.

It is undoubtedly true that the Sutta is an excellent moral foundation for children. But that is just a beginning. The Sutta also is a cultural, moral and spiritual compass for guiding the ship of life through the stormy ocean of existence to the safe final haven of the

Further Shore. At every step in life, at every stage and under all circumstances, the Sutta has practical advice to offer, advice which if followed may be expected to lead to the effective solution of many complicated problems. The Sutta provides unfailing guidance not only to a child at school or to youngsters in their teens but also to grown-ups, no matter what age and what their status or work, race or nation, creed or education. Homes, schools, universities, law courts, hospitals, factories, monasteries, government and business offices, laboratories and all the other places of human activity can derive substantial benefit from the teachings of the Mahā Maṅgala Sutta. A poor and humble person may gain from the practice of these golden precepts even more than a wealthy man. A prime minister may benefit as much as any humble citizen, a new *sāmaṇera* (novice) as much as a senior Bhikkhu, a labourer in the field as much as a king on his throne, a school teacher, a compounder or a petition-writer as much as a professor or a doctor or a pleader. The Sutta is a general prescription most excellent for the difficulties of everyone, for alleviating moral decay and for mending the spiritual fractures of all men and women of all times and places, of all races and religions. Such is its grandeur! Such is the glory of this short discourse which may rightly be designated a universal panacea.

In the practical application of the teachings of the Sutta is the effective solution of all problems whether personal or domestic, private or public, national or international. The benefit, however, is in accordance with the degree of practice, which if habitual leads to a mental state in which it is natural to distinguish between the *maṅgala* and the *amaṅgala,*[15] practices and to flow only with the former according with one's practice.

Though the Sutta is a part of the Buddhist canon, its contents breathe such a harmonious air that they are the property of the whole human race. In its sublime teaching the distinctions of creed, race and nationality vanish and the rigid frontiers of religion melt away, making the peoples of the human race seem as members of one undivided family. Bound together by common problems and by the urge to find their solutions, mankind is certain to benefit from the wisdom enshrined in the Sutta.

The teachings of the Sutta are an excellent instrument for conditioning humanity in the direction of intellectual clarity and emotional purity towards efficiency in work and amity in human relationship. The world today sorely needs such advice. Shaken by the two worst wars in history and tormented by the possibility of a third one, worse than any before, most of the world's peoples today are naturally thirsting for peace. To quench this thirst, apart from suitable economic readjustments, intellectual honesty and emotional strength are essential. They are of paramount importance; in fact, much more important than the deluded trust in the strength of armies and the hollow hope in the potency of atomic and hydrogen bombs and other devilish weapons. It is our experience that wars, far from solving the problems causing them, create more unsolvable problems in their wake. To go to war heedlessly is madness and a suicidal policy. Besides the fact of coming to blows is evidently an admission of the moral and intellectual bankruptcy among those nations which fight.

---

15. I.e., inauspicious, evil and not commendable.

The trouble with the world today is more a matter of its individual human inhabitants than the state of the objective world. The causes of these troubles are greed, hatred and delusion. These fires within manifest as conflicts without, unleashing manifold sufferings.

There can be no peace without moral and intellectual concord among mankind. There can be no real love in human relationships so long as the fires of hate, dishonesty, anger and greed fiercely burn in the human heart. Like war, peace has to be won. The Mahā Maṅgala Sutta of the Buddha shows the way to do it. It shows the way of genuine victory through non-violence and real love. Rather than conquering thousands and millions in battle, the Buddha teaches the conquest of self through self-culture and self-control. This is a victory well worth winning! It leads to peace—its substance is unshakable happiness and its fruit, perfect security.

Effective victory over self illumines every sphere of life: personal, family, social, national and international; also physical, mental, moral and spiritual. Thus the Mahā Maṅgala Sutta deals with the harmonious development of the whole man in his total environment.

There are thirty-eight *maṅgalas* or acts of blessedness, each of which is designated the "best" or the "highest." In view of the fact that these acts include such different spheres as worldly pursuits, family life, religious practices and spiritual ideals, it may reasonably be asked as to why all of these are each called the best, as *maṅgalam-uttamaṃ*.

The Sutta deals with personal life as a whole. But, as life has different stages, different precepts condition each stage towards a wholesome state. Step by step the evolution of the individual proceeds, each step having some acts or blessings as unique to itself. As the individual progresses, his attention increases and his outlook is focused on different ends. On looking back he may well feel like a mature person looking at the toys of his childhood. Certainly, what was highest or best then is not so for him now. And it is true too that what he regards as the highest or the best will be rejected by a child. At the different stages of life different counsels are needed, the best for each phase of the journey. Just as man going off to market with a bag of charcoal on his back, on finding wool discards the charcoal, on finding silver discards wool, on finding gold discards silver, on finding diamonds discards gold and on finding the secret of enduring happiness discards everything else, so too we successively shift the level of our outlook, focusing our consciousness to ideals higher and higher till the highest is reached.

The Mahā Maṅgala Sutta gives the best counsel for each stage of life; it is thus that worldly felicity and spiritual bliss cease to be conflicting ideals. Every ideal that is good is "best" in its own place. That is why each of the thirty-eight Blessings is the "highest" and the "best."

So great is the importance of the Mahā Maṅgala Sutta that if one had to face a situation where it was necessary to surrender all the teachings of the Buddha except a single discourse, one would do well to hold on to the Mahā Maṅgala Sutta. Having this as a possession it would be possible, even quite easy, to reconstruct the entire teachings of the Buddha. This opinion is ventured to emphasize vividly the practical value of the sublime Sutta, which provides an all-round and unfailing guidance for worldly promotion and spiritual salvation.

The understanding and proper practice of the Sutta would help the world more towards prosperity, moral excellence, harmony, peace, happiness and spiritual glory, than a hundred international conferences.

Because man has become cleverer than wiser, he has to face endless trouble today. Unless his cleverness is properly balanced by wisdom, there is every danger of his being wiped out of existence, not unlike the fate suffered by a monkey recklessly playing with a flaming cigarette lighter surrounded by open drums of gasoline. Certainly there is enough of the monkey still in man. The Mahā Maṅgala Sutta holds out the promise of evolving man towards true humanity. It makes of him a complete personality, physically healthy, vocationally efficient, intellectually brilliant, socially benevolent, culturally talented, morally wholesome, materially resplendent and spiritually unexcelled.

The Mahā Maṅgala Sutta is truly the

HOPE OF THE WORLD

May all be well and happy!

—§§§—

THE BUDDHIST PUBLICATION SOCIETY

The BPS is an approved charity dedicated to making known the Teaching of the Buddha, which has a vital message for all people.

Founded in 1958, the BPS has published a wide variety of books and booklets covering a great range of topics. Its publications include accurate annotated translations of the Buddha's discourses, standard reference works, as well as original contemporary expositions of Buddhist thought and practice. These works present Buddhism as it truly is—a dynamic force which has influenced receptive minds for the past 2500 years and is still as relevant today as it was when it first arose.

You can support the BPS by becoming a member. All members receive the biannual membership book and are entitled to discounts on BPS books.

For more information about the BPS and our publications, please visit our website, or write an e-mail, or a letter to the:

Administrative Secretary
Buddhist Publication Society
P.O. Box 61
54 Sangharaja Mawatha
Kandy • Sri Lanka

E-mail: bps@bps.lk
web site: http://www.bps.lk
Tel: 0094 81 223 7283 • Fax: 0094 81 222 3679